FOODS OF THE SOUTHWEST
INDIAN NATIONS

FOODS OF THE SOUTHWEST

INDIAN NATIONS

TRADITIONAL & CONTEMPORARY
NATIVE AMERICAN RECIPES

LOIS ELLEN FRANK

CULINARY ADVISORS
WALTER WHITEWATER
SAM ETHERIDGE

TEN SPEED PRESS
Berkeley

Author's note: Foods in this book may be unfamiliar, especially to those who have never been to the Southwest. I urge readers to be absolutely certain to identify wild edible plants, flowers, and herbs before eating them and to adhere to any special instructions or warnings I have included in the recipes. Most states have laws against the removal of some of their native plants from their natural habitat and on the collection of seeds and fruits. Check regulations in your own state for the law and to see if any plants are protected or endangered before harvesting anything that grows in the wild. This ensures and protects these plants and makes them available for future generations. I also suggest that inexperienced hunters purchase game meats from a butcher or meat supplier, as wild animals may carry disease.

Copyright © 2002 by Lois Ellen Frank
Photographs copyright © 2002 by Lois Ellen Frank

Originally published in the United States by Clarkson Potter, New York, in 1991.

Library of Congress Cataloging-in-Publication Data
Frank, Lois Ellen.
Foods of the Southwest Indian nations : traditional & contemporary
Native American recipes / Lois Ellen Frank ; culinary advisors,
Walter Whitewater, Sam Etheridge ; design by Jennifer Barry.
p.   cm.
1. Indian cookery. 2. Cookery, American—Southwestern style.
3. Indians of North America—Food—Southwest, New. I. Title.
TX715.F8354   2002
641.59'297—dc21   2002002094

ISBN-13: 978-1-58008-398-0

Printed in China

Cover and Interior Design by Jennifer Barry Design, Sausalito, CA
Layout Production, Kristen Wurz

14 13 12 11 10 9 8 7 6 5

First Ten Speed Press Edition

Photograph page 8: Walter Whitewater, Diné (Navajo) from Pinon, Arizona.

*To the Native elders, especially the women who have
shared many of their food ways, opened their homes and hearts,
and who carry the knowledge of their cultural traditions.
May we ask questions and learn all that we can from our elders,
for they are the ones that possess knowledge.*

*To my grandmothers,
Grandma Liz and Nana Rose who have gone on*

*And to my family:
my mother, Jeanne
my father, Henry, and stepmother, Arlene
my sister, Cynthia
and my brothers, Gregory and Glenn*

*And to Walter's grandmother,
Susie Whitewater Begay (Diné)*

ACKNOWLEDGMENTS

Many more people than I ever could have imagined helped me in the completion of this book. I am so grateful to each and every one of them for their support.

The spirit of this book comes from the Indian women who patiently taught me how to make some of the recipes and demonstrated their cooking techniques for traditional dishes.

I would like to express my deepest gratitude to the following people:

Walter Whitewater for his culinary advice, for helping test all the recipes for this book, and his assistance on the photographs—both the food shots in the studio and many of the people shots on location. He worked many tireless hours on the completion of this book.

Sam Etheridge for his culinary advice and for helping test and shoot many of the meat recipes.

John Sedlar for his culinary expertise on the adaptation of the original recipes to the first manuscript.

My sister, Cynthia J. Frank, for helping to write the original manuscript for this book and to organize my thoughts so that they could be put into words in the first edition.

Susan Southcott and Norman Stewart, two of the most talented food stylists who helped with the food styling of the original photographs from the first edition.

Mark Miller for writing the foreword to this book, and all the collaborations and projects we have worked on over the years.

Dr. Beverly Singer, for writing the foreword to this book as a representation of Native Peoples.

My advisor and head of my committee at the University of New Mexico, Dr. Mari Lyn Salvador for her help and support. She helped me to crystallize my thoughts and present them in this book in a clear and concise way.

Dr. Karl Schwerin, member of my committee at UNM, who helped with all of the botanical names and information on many of the native foods of the Southwest and their histories.

Annie Nelson, my editor at Ten Speed Press, for her patience and help on the text of this book.

Jenny Barry for her beautiful design work on this book.

Thanks to the following Native American people who opened up their hearts and their homes, both on and off the reservations. Each has helped in a multitude of ways. Their names and tribal affiliations are:

Walter Whitewater and his family, Grandma Susie; Thomas Mike; Linda Begay; her children Courtney and Cassandra; and granddaughter, Mara Fiona (*Diné from Pinon, Arizona*).

And Walter's daughter, Calandra Willie (*Diné from Seba, Arizona*).

Rita and George Yazzie, their daughter Ann-Marie, and her children, Tiffany and Tim Junior (*Diné from Pinon, Arizona*).

Maggie Begay; Francine Yeigh; her daughter, Yvette Griswold; Joe and Emily Begay, and their children (*Diné from Pinon, Arizona*).

Grandma Louise Begaye; her son, Paul C. Begaye Tohlakai, and all her other children, their spouses, and their children (*Diné from Pinon, Arizona*).

Lola and Billy Hayes (*Whittier, California and Pinon, Arizona*).

Juanita Tiger Kavena and her wonderful family: Wilmer, Maria, Tita, Chibbon, Alisha, Natyo, Lisa, and the late Tracy (*Hopi from First Mesa, Arizona*).

E.J. Satala; his late parents, Granny and Grampa; his sister, Hazel; his son, Spike; and all the members of the Honanie family (*Hopi from Polacca, Arizona*).

Genevieve Kaursgowva (*Hopi from Hotevilla, Arizona*).

Richard and Margie Mermejo and all of their family, children, and grandchildren (*Picuris Pueblo, New Mexico*).

Ann Taliman (*Santa Clara Pueblo, New Mexico*).

Charlotte and Phillip Titla (*Apache from San Carlos, Arizona*).

Del Mar Boni (*San Carlos Apache*) and Gila River (*Pima Reservation*).

Gina Marie Thomas and her daughter, Alisia (*White River Apache, White River, Arizona*).

Sarah H. Adeky and her family (*Ramah Navajo Tribe, Ramah, New Mexico*).

Jolene Eustace-Hanelt (*Zuni and Cochiti Pueblo, Santa Fe, New Mexico*).

Ella Marie Covington (*Tohono O'odham from Tucson, Arizona*).

Tedra Begay (*Diné from Gilbert, Arizona*).

I would also like to show my appreciation to the following tribes, Pueblos, and people for their participation in and contributions to this book:

John Bowannie and Lena Jaramillo, Cochiti Pueblo, Cochiti, New Mexico. Lucille Watahomigie, Hualapai Reservation, Peach Springs, Arizona. Lupita S. Garcia; Juanita K. Jojola; Teddy Lente; and Anita S. Abeita, Isleta Pueblo, Isleta, New Mexico. Betty Johnson and Maria Elena Roybal, Isleta Pueblo, Isleta, New Mexico. Inez Toya and Angie Trujillo, Jemez Pueblo, Jemez, New Mexico. Margaret Archuleta and Mary Ann Martinez, Picuris Pueblo, Penasco, New Mexico. Frank Gutierrez, Janice Naranjo, and Tessie Naranjo, Santa Clara Pueblo, Española, New Mexico. Dr. Donald S. Heany and Annabel Eagle, Southern Ute Tribe, Ignacio, Colorado. Lillian Romero, Taos Pueblo, Taos, New Mexico. Sue Dorame, Tesuque Pueblo, Tesuque, New Mexico.

My professors at UNM, the late Dr. Alfonso Ortiz, Dr. Keith Basso, Dr. Les Field, and Dr. Carole Nagengast for teaching me about methods and how to use an academic approach to the subject of food and Native Peoples.

Sheila LaPlante and Tony Nethery for their help testing some of the recipes in this book.

Melina Salvador for her support and for reminding me to laugh.

Sean C. Casey for coming into my life and encouraging me during the completion of this book.

To all the many gallery owners and stores, who through their generosity, allowed me to use numerous artifacts and plates for the photographs and offered their premises for on-location shoots. Thank you.

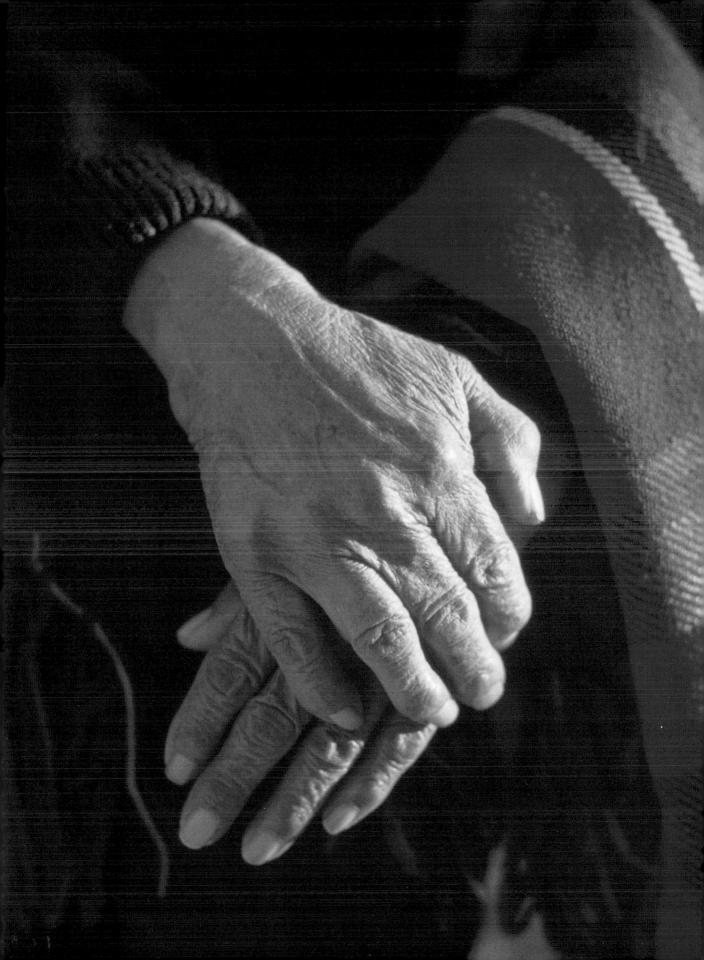

CONTENTS

FOREWORD

The first edition of Lois Frank's *Native American Cooking* came out at a time when America was just waking up to its own culinary history. As chefs across the country rushed to investigate regional differences in American cuisine, from Creole to California cuisine, it became clear that many of these styles were inspired by Native American cooking traditions and methods—one of the reasons that studying the history of Native American cooking is so important today. With their rich history of farming, plant usage and diversification, and careful natural observations, Native Americans were America's first great cooks.

Lois has spent a lifetime studying the history, culinary culture, and complexities of Native American food and its people, and in doing so has developed a deep understanding of the complex cultural importance of food and how it unites people to the land and the rest of the natural world. As an accomplished photographer, Lois is able to capture the diversity of people and their heritages in her images. She also uses her camera to document the wonders of a seemingly simple food like corn. She and I have traveled from the Peabody Museum in Boston to the wilds of the Andes and have gone on exotic journeys through the grasslands of Mexico, where the first domesticated corn was grown. We visited a 500-year-old cornfield in the mountains of Oaxaca, where the corn stalks grew to more than 20 feet tall. She has traveled over the mountains of Bolivia searching for ancient corn recipes, taking photos of corns that haven't been seen by the modern world. Like the Southwest Indian Nations themselves, the food of the region has a great story to tell, and nobody tells that story better than Lois. She weaves together seamlessly the story of the food and the people, and her years of living among Native Americans and her education in anthropology give her work a depth that is unparalleled.

In this new edition of her book, Lois brings us close to the beauty and simplicity of Native American cooking. Although the roots of the cuisine that she presents are ancient, the recipes in this book are timeless. Recipes for stews and dumplings—examples of the original "comfort foods"—reflect a modern appreciation for fresh herbs and spices. And the use of traditional Native American foods, like elk, rabbit, and other wild game, as well as prickly pear and piñons, reflect current chefs' search for regional and seasonal ingredients.

Whether you are an avid fan of Southwest or Native American cooking or just a casual weekend cook, the following recipes will fascinate you and your friends with the diverse tastes and aromas of the cuisine. These recipes tell the story of the origins of the foods that we eat and enjoy today.

—Mark Miller, chef/owner, Coyote Café, Santa Fe, New Mexico

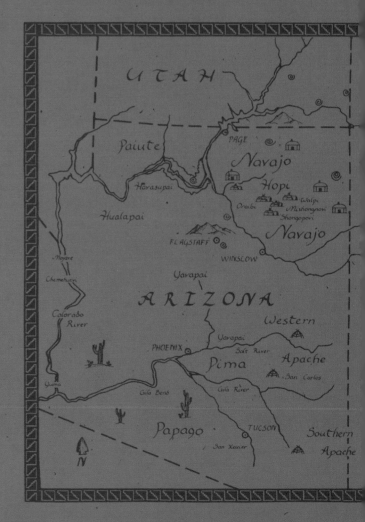

FOOD WAYS AND INDIAN IMAGES

Lois Ellen Frank has fulfilled an impressive and inquisitive assignment about foods eaten and prepared by Indian Nations in the American Southwest. Through her photographs and words, Frank shares an endowed history of American Indians as agricultural and wild game specialists and further demonstrates their ingenuity as cooks. Photographing images that honor and respect the foods eaten by Native peoples in the Southwest is a more complex task than one might think at the outset. Frank's accomplishment in this project rests in her skill as a gifted photographer combined with her sincerity in working with the subject of food and Indians upon which she focuses fondly.

Photographs of American Indians are trademarks in the history of America and in particular, Indians in the Southwest have been celebrated in photographs depicting us in our original homelands usually in colorful regalia demonstrating our art and life ways in magazine spreads. There is a special character and a settled quality of life associated with living in the arid desert and mountains of the Southwestern United States but the effects of over a hundred years of tourism have made the native populations in the region resistant to being photographed for commercial purposes. Moreover, the private and personal lives of the Diné (Navajo), Indé (Apache), Pueblo, O'odham, and Nahuatl are naturally reserved for family and community sharing which they choose to share or not with outsiders today. That said, Lois Ellen Frank is a very special person with whom many indigenous families have accepted and among other things shared their friendship and food recipes. In turn, with their permission Frank shares with us a love of food and of things "Indian" which adds to our knowledge and promotes respect concurrently.

It is exciting to witness accommodation and change in native recipes as illustrated by Frank, for alongside the ancient corn recipes of Chaquewa (corn porridge) and Piki bread one can also find the innovation of Cornsicles with shrimp and oregano. This food styling extends a new dimension to native cooking that gives a modern twist to established ideas. In this regard, Frank provides excellent chapter introductions that discuss and give context to the long-held beliefs and practices associated with Indian food ways. Finally, her careful photographic depiction of very modern images of prepared dishes also compliment and respect Indian beliefs about food. For many centuries Indian people have sought a healthy outlook and balance with the natural world and in this beautiful volume one will experience this association with the essence for eating—to live life from within rather than outside of ourselves.

—*Beverly R. Singer, Ph.D. (Santa Clara Pueblo/Diné), Director, Alfonso Ortiz Center for Intercultural Studies, Department of Anthropology, University of New Mexico*

PREFACE

When I graduated from Brooks Institute of Photography in Santa Barbara, California, I was asked to give a speech at the commencement. Given this special opportunity, I wanted to reach out to every person there and explain my feelings about photography, especially about how the images we produce have an impact on the people that view them. We can use our photographic images to move people, to make them think, to influence their decisions, and to represent people and their ways of life.

After I spoke, the renowned photographer Ernst Haas gave a speech. Although I had never met him before, his vision of what it is to be a photographer was very similar to mine. It was then that I knew Ernst Haas would become a mentor and a friend. As I got to know Ernst better, he encouraged me to share many of my own ideas with him. To my dismay, he questioned some of the work I was doing. "If this is not the poetry from inside your heart," he asked, "then what is it? Is this the message you want to give to others?" I had no answer. After years of educating myself in a field I deeply loved, I was completely lost.

Ernst believed that in order to express yourself through an art form you must allow your uninhibited childlike feelings to surface, and you must be able to capture those images in pure form. "Quite often," he explained, "I see people photographing things just to make money. When they finally reach a point in their lives when they have time to be creative, they have forgotten what it is that they wanted to express in the first place." It was at this point that I really began to search for the message I wanted to convey through my own photography, a search that has continued ever since.

My family ancestry is mixed. On my mother's side I am a European blend, mostly English, and Kiowa, and on my father's side I am Sephardic and German Jewish—my ancestors from Europe entered this country in 1640 on the third *Mayflower* trip, and my father's family entered through Ellis Island, New York, and settled in Brooklyn. I wasn't raised with Indian traditions, and I never knew my Kiowa grandfather; however, my mother used to tell me stories, and my Native American heritage was something that I wanted to know about.

I have spent many years visiting and living on Southwestern Indian reservations. I learned from the elders where to find, how to harvest, and how to prepare many Native American foods from different nations. The elders taught me traditional methods of cooking as well as new approaches. I worked with several generations of women, side by side, in a single household, as well as with contemporary Native chefs, both women and men, who worked in restaurants. Throughout this whole process of learning about Native foods, I have photographed many of the people and the food preparation techniques, and cooked for hundreds of people during Feasts, festivities, and ceremonies. I have become like a daughter to some families and am expected to help with preparing food and serving the invited guests year after year. It has been a privilege and an honor to be welcomed into so many households.

In 1991, I moved from Los Angeles, California, to Santa Fe, New Mexico. Living in the Southwest has enabled me to work closely with many people from the reservations and Pueblos of the region. After the release of my first book on Native American foods in 1991, I, along with several other young chefs—Walter Whitewater, Jeff Koscomb, and Aland Humphries—toured the United States cooking many of these foods at restaurants. The ingredients we couldn't get in the cities we traveled to, we harvested and brought ourselves. We traveled with freshly harvested prickly pears, acorn nuts, and Indian tea, to name a few ingredients, and cooked them in some of the finest restaurants in the United States. The chefs and kitchen staffs were as excited as we were and helped in all stages of preparing these Native American menus. We served the food to an audience that was as diverse as the Southwestern landscape from which it came. They were surprised at the subtlety of Native American cuisine. We received the highest of praise then, much as we do now.

In 1996, I reentered academia at the University of New Mexico (UNM), and I received my master's degree in cultural anthropology in 1999. It was a difficult transition for me to go back to being a full-time student after being absent from the educational arena since receiving my bachelor's degree from Brooks Institute in 1985. Many of my professors at UNM were very supportive of my endeavors and research on traditional foods, plants, and herbs of Native Peoples from the Southwest, and my work in Mexico and South America.

I am presently enrolled in the Ph.D. program at the University of New Mexico, where I continue to conduct research on foods, including medicinal and spiritual plants, and to work on projects focusing on the importance of foods among Indigenous Peoples of the Americas. My thesis will examine contemporary chefs, how they have been influenced by Native foods and cultures of the Southwest, and what this means in terms of their own identity and expression of their foods today.

Academia has given me a new perspective on how to represent other peoples and their foods. It has given me the opportunity to take full responsibility for these representations and to collaborate with people from each community I represent, giving them a voice in what we say and how we say it. I have made decisions based on this perspective that are reflected in this book. Throughout the book I have used the terms Native American, American Indian, Indigenous, Native, and Native Peoples—all of which people here in the Southwest use to refer to themselves. I have spelled Native names the way the People in the region have asked me to, and I refer to Peoples as they call themselves first, and then provide the names by which they are commonly called by others. Scientific names for many of the plants have been given, as common names of foods and plants vary from region to region. It is my hope that readers will broaden their knowledge and further investigate some of the foods I have presented here.

The spicy red and green peppers that flavor so many Southwestern dishes originated in Mexico. While "chili" is the anglicized spelling of the word based on the Nahuatl word "chilli," I have chosen to spell it using the Spanish "chile," as it is the more common spelling and the form used by most suppliers. In other situations where there is more than one spelling for a specific word, I have chosen the spelling I think most commonly used throughout the Southwest.

It is important to note that there are many more recipes from the peoples of this vast region that I have not been able to include. What I offer here is a small sampling of the abundance of foods and recipes from the Southwest. I am attempting to represent many different and diverse nations with a broad range of customs, languages, and beliefs. If any information has been excluded or has offended any of the peoples I am attempting to represent, it has not been intentional.

The foods I write about were not only important in the past but are also crucial to the future. We are finding that Native foods are vitally important to the health and well-being of the Indigenous peoples from this region. These food traditions are very much alive today, and their importance is being realized by all of the different cultural groups now sharing the Southwest. In addition to rediscovering the nutritional benefits of these desert foods, we have also begun to honor their heritage. Whether you actually gather and cook some of these foods or just read about the recipes, I hope that the knowledge of how important these foods are will help you to appreciate more fully the Southwest and the Indian Nations that live here.

In the tradition of the Native American people, a percentage of royalties from this book will be donated to help better the futures of Native American children through a scholarship and intern fund and to further intercultural studies. I encourage you to make donations as well. Individual donations can be made to the Alfonso Ortiz Center for Intercultural Studies through the Department of Anthropology at the University of New Mexico. Contributions to the fund are tax deductible.

Finally, I hope this book inspires others—both Native and non-Native—to continue to pursue knowledge of the foods from not only the Southwest Indian Nations, but other Nations as well.

—*Lois Ellen Frank*

NATIVE AMERICANS have lived on this land since before history's written records, far beyond any living memory. The story of the people in the Southwest and the story of this place is one story. One cannot think of this place and not think of its people. Indigenous people of the Southwest are as diverse as the land they live on. Nevertheless, they share the belief that food is important beyond physical sustenance. The acts of hunting, growing, gathering, cooking, and eating take on a spiritual aspect akin to prayer. The relationship between the land and its people is sacred.

"When we talk about place—we talk about Earth and we have to consider what's under the Earth, what's on the Earth, what's above the Earth. The people were the Anasazi who lived here. There are ruins and remains of them. The people when they hunted would run herds of game through these lands and kill the animals—it has a history of being a ground where animals sacrificed themselves for the good of the people. The ancient culture that lived here had their ceremonies. They greeted the sun every morning. Now we recognize the power, the spirit that dwells on the land—we see how the wind shifts, where it comes from, and the directions of it." Paul C. Begaye Tohlakai, Navajo elder from Pinon, Arizona, 2000.

Native American artists today express their feelings about the Southwest through their pottery, jewelry, painting, sculpture, and architecture. This sense of place is evoked in a variety of ways and poetic means. Place can be experienced through the oral traditions of the Native people here. Their stories hold and unleash wisdom that embodies memories in manners of voicing, and that animates the sensuality of place as both landscape and soundscape.[i] "American Indians hold their lands—places—as having the highest possible meaning, and all their statements are made with this point in mind."[ii] Their place is who they are; it is expressive of where they came from, where they are now, and where they will go in the future.

Opposite: Gina Marie Thomas (Whiteriver Apache/Akimiel O'odham) making a prayer offering.

The American Southwest is a land of contrasts and diversity. The physical landscape includes extensive mesas, rugged mountains, and low-lying deserts. Within this region one can move from the Yuman, Piman, including the Akimiel O'odham, "Salt River People," and the Tohono O'odham, "Desert People," to the Pueblo farmers who live along the watercourses, from a few hundred feet above sea level to more than 7,000 feet above sea level. Yavapai and Walapai people, known as the "Upland Yumans," and the Athapaskan-speaking Apache and Diné (Navajo) peoples also share this diverse land. The Apache and Diné groups have maintained a somewhat nomadic existence even in contemporary times by raising sheep and cattle.[iii] Three of these four traditions—Piman, Yuman, and Pueblo cultures—developed in the Southwest over ten thousand years. The Apache and Diné are relative newcomers, probably entering the Southwest in the early sixteenth century.[iv]

Interspersed among these contemporary peoples of the Southwest there is also evidence everywhere of its ancient inhabitants. The late Alfonso Ortiz, a renowned anthropologist from the San Juan Pueblo, suggests that some artifacts, like the petroglyphs, date back untold millennia, and others, like potsherds and pit houses, may go back to the time of Christ. With careful observation and precise, sophisticated measurement, celestial movements were used for planting and harvesting, and to judge when to expect rainfall or major migrations of animals. The ancient ones, or Anasazi, as they are called by the Diné, constructed an ingenious seasonal clock called the Sun Dagger in Chaco Canyon. Sun rays striking particular points on a spiral motif etched on a rock wall indicated when to plant, when to harvest, and when the seasons would change. Many of these spiral motifs can still be seen today, etched on rocks throughout the Southwest.

The knowledge of events in this area beyond a few thousand years ago is still far from complete. Imports from Mesoamerica were embraced in diverse ways by the hunting and gathering peoples of the Southwest. These coalesced into four distinctive prehistoric civilizations—Anasazi, Mogollon, Hohokam, and Hakataya.[v] Within the diverse area of the Southwest, a variety of subsistence adaptations was practiced in historic times. Some Peoples cultivated only limited crops, deriving most of their food from wild plant and animal resources. Other groups engaged in irrigation agriculture supplemented by hunting and gathering. Settlement patterns were and are equally diverse.[vi]

Of the peoples living in the northern portion of the Southwest, the Pueblos suffered the most from the early and continued contact with the Spaniards. Coronado visited the Rio Grande Pueblos and Zuni in 1540, and in 1598 the first Spanish colonial capital in New Mexico was established near San Juan Pueblo. During the seventeenth century, missionization was pursued ardently among the Pueblos; the repressive activities enforced by the friars were one of the major factors leading the Pueblos to unite and revolt. The Spanish demanded labor and tribute from the Pueblos and vigorously attempted to suppress Native religions. The Pueblo revolt against the Spanish took place in 1680, and they managed to expel the Spaniards until 1692. Don Diego de Vargas reentered Pueblo country in 1692 and it was not until 1696 that he gained control over the entire Rio Grande Pueblo area.

The Hopi people and the nomadic tribes were more independent during this postrevolutionary period and the period that followed. In 1846, the United States took control of the portion of the Southwest north of the Rio Grande and began campaigns to settle the nomadic tribes on reservations. By 1863, the Mescalero Apache had fled into Mexico or were imprisoned at Fort Sumner. Most of the Diné were forced to join them there in 1864. To this day, Diné people refer to their journey to Fort Sumner as the tragic Long Walk. After four years, the Diné were allowed to return to their homeland, and four reservations were set aside for the various bands of Apaches.[vii] Other native groups in the Southwest have also retained portions of their homelands, though the struggle to keep these lands has been a continuous one.

The history of the Southwest has been a long and sometimes harsh one. However, even with outside influences and external pressures, these Pueblo communities have somehow maintained their way of life. The Pueblos maintained their ceremonial life out of view of the Spaniards, while adopting the veneer of Roman Catholicism. They held onto an intensive horticulture system, an elaborate ceremonial cycle, and a cohesive social organization—in villages of adobe and stone, most of which are situated along the Rio Grande.

Central to this lifestyle is farming and the major crop, corn. Today, corn is still vital and sacred to the Pueblos. Other cultivated foods, such as chiles, squash, beans, tomatoes, melons, peaches, apricots, and apples, are grown in addition to corn in many Pueblo gardens. Some of these plants have been cultivated for thousands of years here in the Southwest, and others were brought north by the Spanish.

Wild plants are also gathered and harvested and used as food and medicine and for spiritual purposes. Game is hunted, and many of the animals are honored by the performance of ceremonial Winter Animal Dances. Buffalo, deer, elk, and bighorn sheep are honored by these dances, and thanks are given to the animals. Other foods have also become a part of the Pueblo diet, including wheat, pork, lamb, and beef, all of which were introduced by the Spanish.

The land of the Diné does not differ much from that of the Pueblos. The two peoples differ, however, in how they live on the land. The Diné, unlike the Pueblos, remain thinly spread out within the canyons, at the bases of cliffs, and in and around mesas. Many have become quite successful cultivators and grow corn, beans, squash, chiles, and melons using the dry-farming method, but sheepherding and raising cattle is primary for many of the traditional Diné living on the reservation today. Meat is central to most meals, and frybread or some other kind of bread is served with almost every meal. Many women still make frybread daily, but cooking is increasingly shared by men and women.

Many Apache live dispersed on mountainous reservations in central Arizona and New Mexico. In Arizona, they are the guardians of the watersheds to some of the major feeder streams of rivers in the Southwest. In New Mexico, they live to the north and to the south of the Pueblo people. Still somewhat nomadic, some Apache raise cattle and sheep and live in a ranchlike setting. Corn is important not only as a food source, but also because its pollen is used in every girl's coming-of-age ceremony. Acorns are regularly gathered each season, as are some of the wild fruits and berries of the regions. Men hunt deer in the fall, and in some regions to the north elk is also hunted. Delicious stews are prepared upon the return of the hunters with fresh game. The Apaches' gathering techniques are reflected in their baskets, deep and cone shaped, which are good for harvesting wild foods and carrying them back to camp.

The Hopi people of northern Arizona are known for their blue corn. They still plant fields of corn, with seeds planted up to 18 inches deep, and are able to produce crops with no irrigation at all. Many traditional corn dishes are prepared today much as they have been prepared for centuries. The Hopi have many terraced gardens growing beans, squash, chiles, and tomatoes, as well as orchards producing apricots, peaches, and plums, also without any irrigation. Their rich ceremonial cycle centers primarily around the planting of their crops and the spirits that bring rain.

The Havasupais, or "Blue-Green Water People," have tended farms in the Grand Canyon of the Colorado River for hundreds of years. Their original gardens were once farms in what became the Grand Canyon National Park. Today farming is practiced only in Havasu Canyon. They grow a variety of field and tree crops, and their peaches are especially renowned. The crops are irrigated by Havasu Creek, which flows on to form the beautiful and famous waterfalls. There is even a town named Peach Springs, located in Arizona just inside the Hualapai reservation borders.

The homeland of the Akimiel O'odham and the Tohono O'odham stretches from Phoenix, Arizona, to east central Sonora, Mexico. It includes some of the hottest, driest areas of North America. They have given us some of the world's most drought-hardy, heat-tolerant, and alkali-adapted crops. In addition to the selections of corn, tepary beans, and cushaw squash grown with the summer rains, the Akimiel and Tohono also developed agriculture using floodwater or runoff in temperatures consistently exceeding 100 degrees. The Tohono O'odham in and around the Tucson, Arizona, area harvest the fruit of the giant saguaro cactus every summer when the fruits are ripe. The harvest of this fruit is very important to the Tohono O'odham and the Akimiel O'odham people, and its importance is reflected in many stories from their oral traditions.

The Southwestern peoples and their traditions are very much alive today. Each group practices varying farming and planting techniques that have been handed down from generation to generation to suit the environments in which they live. Some foods are prepared as they have been for hundreds of years, while other foods incorporate contemporary ingredients and utensils. Knowledge is passed down orally. Grandparents teach children, whether they are deer hunting, acorn hunting, or gathering wild plants. Many elements of American Indian life are passed down like this.[viii]

What makes Native food traditions unique is the respect for the bounty enjoyed by the people. Among many Native Peoples of the Southwest nothing is taken for granted. Offerings are made to corn plants, often in the form of a song or prayer. These songs and offerings are believed to help the plants to grow and be productive.

I grow corn every year, and have now for years. Last year when one of my nieces, Cassandra, who is ten, was visiting from Pinon, Arizona, on the Diné reservation saw the young corn plants outside the windows of my house. She found a clay corn figurine shaped like one of the deities from the Yucatan that I had been given by some friends in Mexico. Without even thinking, she placed the figurine in one of the open windows in the living room so it could face the corn plants. When I asked her why she did that, she responded that she thought this clay figure could sing to my corn plants and help them to grow. So there it sat for weeks, quietly singing its songs to the corn plants to help them grow.

Many people today still revere corn. Some greet the rising sun every morning with an offering of cornmeal or corn pollen. Words are spoken acknowledging a new day, and thanks are given for the blessings that might be bestowed.

Animals are honored, too, through dances and in ceremonies. Native American hunts are never done for sport, but rather game is hunted for its meat and skins. This respect for the natural balance of things is basic to Native American belief.

Similarly, Native People harvest only what is needed of native plants. What is taken at one time will be used for that year or season, and some is always left to propagate more for others in the future. Nothing is wasted. Leftover foods, whether the seeds of fruit or skins of a vegetable, are returned to the earth, sometimes in the form of compost and sometimes as food for livestock. Wild plants are taken only when there is an abundance of that plant in a particular area, and then the unused parts are returned to the earth as well.

Cooking has become a viable career option for young Native Americans and is being practiced professionally not only by women but also by men. Some of these native chefs are now cooking in restaurants, producing some delicious dishes based on their traditional knowledge and practices. This is not only happening in the Southwest, but also in other regions of the United States.

Walter Whitewater, who was one of the culinary advisors for this book, is one example. Although he grew up in a family where primarily the women are cooks, Walter decided to become a chef. As a traditional Diné, he follows many of his customary ways, and yet he has cooked in some of the finest restaurant kitchens in the Santa Fe area. He takes off from his cooking obligations to go home every summer for several weeks and fulfills his ceremonial obligations, with full support of his restaurant colleagues. Walter has been a major part of this book, not only in helping with the preparation of the foods, but also in the photographs you will see throughout.

He has toured with me in the past, cooking throughout the United States and collaborating on Southwestern American Indian menus that have received the highest praise. What is so different about these foods and some of the menus is the way in which we have served them. Any wild foods that have been taken from the Southwest to be served in the restaurants have been returned to where they were harvested, with thanks. For example, when prickly pear cactus was harvested in southern Arizona and taken to the East Coast to make a prickly pear sorbet, the skins and seeds were bagged and returned to where they came from.

Contemporary kitchens and chefs are looking to Native farmers and cooks for new ideas and techniques. Many are working side by side, especially here in New Mexico. Farmers are growing what the restaurants need, each member of the partnership benefiting equally from the collaborative effort. Individual tribes are opening their own restaurants on their Pueblos, as well as opening high-end contemporary restaurants in the casinos, which are emerging throughout the Southwest.

Organizations, such as the nonprofit Native Seeds/ SEARCH in Tucson, Arizona, cofounded by Gary Nabhan, an ethnobiologist, are working with Native farmers throughout the Southwest and northern Mexico to conserve traditional food plants and document their associated folklore. Native Seeds/SEARCH conserves, distributes, and documents the adapted and diverse varieties of agricultural seeds and their wild relatives and provides educational information regarding the role these seeds play in cultures of the Southwest and northern Mexico. They promote the use of these ancient crops while working with the communities that use them.

Traditional farmers are a stabilizing force in many Native American communities. They preserve historic seeds adapted to local conditions, keep traditional agricultural and culinary practices alive, donate crops for ceremonies and feast days, and feed extended families from their fields.

Today, there are numerous ethnobotanists, ethnobiologists, anthropologists, and other scientists working side by side with Native communities on agricultural practices, wild food sources, and traditional diets. Work done among the Tohono and Akimiel O'odham Peoples has proven that straying from traditional diets, which include many cacti and native food plants of their region, has resulted in one of the highest rates of diabetes of any ethnic group in the country.[ix] This problem is believed to be directly related to contemporary diets in which there is an absence of important traditional foods that help regulate sugar absorption and stabilize blood sugar. Education programs have helped many people in this area.

Chefs are also taking initiative, contracting specific amounts of crops to be produced in a given season. This chef-farmer connection sustains both the farmer, who is ensured a stable income, and the chef, who has access to delicious organic foods to be served in his or her restaurant.

In schools, programs have been initiated in which culinary professionals emphasize the importance of choosing healthy foods that are good to eat. Traditions, culture, and history are a part of every lesson.[x] Cooking schools are also teaching classes to adults that support this theme. They advocate buying Native food products, which support remote and local communities.

We are now in a new time. Communities are becoming more educated and making decisions that will benefit their children and their children's children.

We need to get young people rejuvenated again, make them proud of their food traditions. Life is still going on; our culture and our food ways are not dead. They live inside each of us. Every time we prepare food as our elders did, we carry on these traditions. We need to listen to our elders, and learn as much as we can, so that we can pass these ways onto our own children and share them with other people outside our own communities as well.[xi]

People are looking toward Native communities for knowledge that will help us better understand sustainability and farming techniques of many traditional foods. I feel honored and privileged to have worked with so many Native cooks in the preparation of this book.

The eating habits of the Southwestern tribes follow the seasons closely. As a result, unlike the European approach to dining, in which meals are composed of several courses that embrace all the basic food groups, traditional meals tend to rely on the staples that are available at any particular time of year. To reflect such an approach to eating, this book is organized not by courses but rather by the main categories of foods Southwest Native Peoples eat. There are separate chapters on corn, the most important staple; chiles, which are almost synonymous with the Southwest; vine grown vegetables and fruits such as squashes and tomatoes; a Native harvest of wild fruits and greens; legumes, nuts, and seeds; and game birds, meats, and fish. Within each of these sections, you'll find recipes for a number or different courses—appetizers, soups, salads, main courses, side dishes, and desserts—from which you can compose a meal that appeals to your own tastes and traditions.

I have not separated the recipes by tribe, but rather integrated them into the appropriate ingredient section. Thus you'll find a variety of influences from many of the Southwestern tribes and Pueblos throughout the book. Rather than being a representation of all the foods from all the tribes and Pueblos of the Southwest, this book is a sampling of recipes that have been graciously shared with me by many Native cooks.

Any adaptations I have made have been done with the sole purpose of making the recipes in this book accessible to as wide an audience as possible. Throughout this book I strive to respect the inherent qualities of the Native American recipes.

CORN

THE ESSENCE OF LIFE

WHETHER we call it corn, Indian corn, maize or *zea mays,* it is all the same thing. This plant, originally an undomesticated wild grass, was turned into a food that would dominate ancient American agriculture for thousands of years and would go on to exert its influence all over the world.

Because of the beauty of corn's color and form many Indigenous peoples of the Americas found time to develop around it a great culture of art, science, literature, and religion. The significance of corn to these cultures' rituals and creation narratives is a part of the story of corn. This story of America is essentially the story of corn and the Native cultures from all over the Americas that developed around it. Corn made cultural development possible by supporting dense concentrations of populations.

Scientists are still debating the actual date of the oldest corn, but evidence from the San Marcos Cave in the Tehuacan Valley of southern Puebla in Mexico suggests it was first cultivated 5,000 to 7,000 years ago.[i]

The domestication of maize was probably a gradual process, eventually taking place over a sizable portion of Mexico and Guatemala, where we find the greatest number of cultivated maize varieties growing today.[ii] Corn is believed to have migrated in two directions, different strains adapting to the climate according to the direction it traveled. The migration routes have been referred to as the Northern Flint and Southern Dent pathways. The Northern Flint pathway took shape in the Rio Grande Valley in about 700 A.D., spreading northward on both sides of the Rocky Mountains. The Southern Dent pathway traveled further to the south into South America.[iii]

Hopi maize is adapted for deep planting in the deserts of the Southwest. Most maize fails to emerge from depths of more than four inches, but this maize is able to sprout from depths of more than eighteen inches, where desert soil retains its moisture.[iv] This variety did not require irrigation, making it ideal for cultivation in the dry, arid Southwest. As the young corn plants grew, the healthiest shoots pushed aside the weaker ones, producing plenty of thriving corn for harvest. "Dry-farming," as this method is called, is actively used today by the Hopi, Diné (Navajo), and some tribes in the desert regions where irrigation is not possible.[v]

There are five major groups of corn: dent, flint, flour, sweet, and pop. They differ in their contents of sugar and starch. Add to this the different colors of the corn plants and the kernels, the different length of time necessary to ripen a crop, and the varying resistance to drought, heat, insects, and diseases, and it becomes easy to imagine the number of varieties of maize.[vi]

In North America, maize was important not only to the Indigenous societies but also to the survival of the first Europeans that settled in the East. Had the Indians not shared their maize with the *Mayflower* Pilgrims, the Pilgrims would have undoubtedly starved during their first terrible winter at Plymouth.[vii]

Corn is, and has been for thousands of years, one of the most important foods in the Native American diet. Considered to be the essence of life, corn is sacred to the people. In fact, prayers are offered to corn, as Mother, at many ceremonial dances. The Tewa-speaking Pueblos speak of two corn mothers who were present before the emergence from a former life within this earth: a white corn mother and a blue corn mother.[viii] In other Pueblos and tribes, corn may be referred to as Maiden or Sister. The focus is slightly different in each instance, but the ideas of corn as mother, enabler, transformer, and healer are components of the same concept.

Throughout the Southwest, there is a recognition that it is necessary to sing the corn to maturity, to sing to it in order for it to grow healthy and productive. The people ask for blessings from the corn, and ask for the corn to come up strong so that it might feed the people and no one will go hungry.[ix]

For Diné people, corn is revered as a food and because it yields pollen, which is important in their heal-

Above: Juanita and Maria Kavena (Hopi) eating piki *bread.*

ing rituals. For the Diné more than any other peoples, corn is a healer.

For the Tohono O'odham, or "Desert People," and the Akimiel O'odham, or "Salt River People," corn is revered and they know it as mother. Again, there were and are songs for all stages of the corn's growth, as well as for the beans and the squash.[x]

Several different varieties and colors of corn, including blue, white, red, yellow, and speckled, are used by Native Americans today. Blue corn, which varies in color from pale blue to almost black, is one of the most important crops. It is used primarily in making baked goods, stews, stuffing, dumplings, and beverages. Recent studies indicate that this variety of corn may have more nutritional value than other types and therefore may help to prevent malnutrition among low-income Indian groups.[xi]

White corn is a major crop on many reservations and Pueblos. It is used in prayer offerings and for making hominy and corn-meal flour, which is used in many traditional recipes. Red corn, ranging in color from light red to deep maroon, is used for baked goods, stews, and traditionally for dye. It is also used to make parched corn, that is, corn that has been roasted so that the kernels are crunchy. Yellow corn is used in stew and is ground into flour or meal for baking. It is often substituted for white corn in cooking because of its greater availability. Sweet corn, best known as corn on the cob, is also grown throughout the Southwest. Speckled corn, which is a combination of all the colors of corn, is used for all kinds of cooking.[xii]

In the past, in order to endure the long, harsh winters, Native Americans dried much of their corn just after harvest, preparing enough to last through two cropless winters. Today, it is common during harvest season to see corn hanging in strands outside adobe houses in the Southwest. There are two methods of drying corn. One is simply to string fresh corn cobs, in their husks, on long yucca threads and hang them outside for several weeks. The other is to bake the cobs before drying, usually in an earthen oven, a process that enhances the corn's flavor.

Many families still use ancient grinding stones for ceremonial corn. Young women still grind corn to the songs of their elders. The Hopi people feel that these stones will never become museum pieces because the process of grinding corn is too sacred. There are many traditional dishes prepared today using corn. *Someviki* (from a Hopi word meaning "tied bread") is prepared from blue corn and placed in dried husks and boiled. *Piki,* a paper-thin cornbread also made from blue or white corn, is prepared on a stone that is passed down from mother to daughter.

A corn roast is also an important social occasion. In a large earthen pit lined with stones a fire is built. After the fire has been fed for several hours, when the sand around the opening of the pit has changed color, corn and cornmeal are pushed into the pit. This is followed by a layer of green corn husks to keep the corn at the bottom from scorching, and to create steam. Up to several hundred ears are placed in the pit, with another layer of corn husks placed at the top to protect the corn. The hole is covered and the corn is roasted until the next morning.

At sunrise the next morning, people gather around the pit and the first ears are eaten in honor of the first sun rays. The rest of the corn is peeled and placed on tarps to dry. Steam still rising from the earthen pit, a prayer to the spirits is offered, usually by the men, and the spirits are asked to join the people in this celebration of the roasted corn. The corn is then transported back to the homes in the village where women string it on yucca strands and place it in the sun to dry.

The miracle of corn is that it grows in the Southwestern desert at all, particularly on some of the arid mesas. But with a history going back thousands of years, it has enabled the Indigenous Peoples of the Southwest to sustain life and to evolve as individual cultures. Corn is Mother. The corn plant itself represents the life cycle of the human being, from the planting of a seed to the growing process to death. The cornstalk dries in the fields, leaving behind new kernels, new seeds of life for future generations to continue the cycle. Corn in the Southwest is the essence of life.

Above: Wilmer Kavena (Hopi) tends to his young corn plants (top). Newly harvested corn being roasted in the traditional way in a large earthen pit right in the field by Thomas Mike (Diné / Navajo) from Pinon, Arizona (bottom).

BAKING SWEET CORN

Native American women have been baking sweet corn for centuries using an ancient method of roasting it in an earthen pit. This method of cooking corn adds a smoky, barbecued flavor to the corn's natural sweetness. Traditionally, corn was dried and shucked after it was baked, so it could be used throughout the winter months. In busier, more modern times, baked corn is frequently frozen in addition to being dried.

It is customary to use white or yellow corn, but blue is often used as well. Any color, however, works just as well in the baking process.

THE TRADITIONAL METHOD

Dig a large pit in the ground, approximately 5 feet deep by 4 feet wide. Line the bottom of the pit with rocks and then with dried wood (piñon, juniper, and cottonwood are most commonly used in the Southwest because of their availability). This process is usually begun in the morning because of the time needed for the pit to be ready. Burn the wood for several hours, adding more as needed, until the earth is warmed and the wood has reduced to glowing embers.

Place a layer of fresh green corn husks and plants (with corn removed) on top of the embers, then a layer of fresh corn ears still in their husks. The layer of corn ears needs to be enough to fill the pit. Top with another layer of green husks and corn plants. For a pit this size, we used several wheelbarrows full of freshly harvested corn ears, which is approximately seventy-five ears of corn. You can make the pit larger or smaller according to how much corn you wish to bake. However, this size pit is a common size used by most families still growing corn today. When the pit is not large enough to bake all the corn ears harvested, this baking process is done several times over the span of about a week during harvest time until all the corn has been roasted in the earthen pit.

Pour two buckets of water into the pit on top of the corn ears and husks. Cover the entire pit with large burlap bags or several blankets and top it with a large piece of canvas. Cover the canvas with some of the dirt from digging the pit.

Allow the corn to bake overnight.

The following morning remove the corn, let cool, shuck the ears, and strip away the silk. Now it can be eaten as is, dried (by being spread outside for several days in fairly warm, dry weather), or frozen (scrape the kernels from the cob and freeze them in plastic bags). If you're lucky enough to be a part of this process of roasting corn, try one of the warm ears once it has been removed from the pit. I've tried white, yellow, and blue corn done this way, and it is really delicious. For me, it is a meal in itself.

INDIAN HOMINY

Almost every tribe and Pueblo throughout the Southwest uses hominy as a base for many of their dishes. Made from dried corn in a variety of colors—white, yellow, blue, and red—hominy can be canned or dried and stored for winter use. Once cooked and the hulls removed, it can also be ground into a meal and used for corn tortillas or tamales, or—most commonly—added to a variety of stews. When sold in certain regions of the Southwest, hominy—canned or dried—is also referred to as posole. *Throughout New Mexico,* posole *can also refer to a cooked dish (page 31). This is the traditional method of making hominy. It was taught to me by Juanita Tiger Kavena from First Mesa in Arizona.*

2¾ cups dried corn kernels, or 1 (1.5-pound) package
    frozen corn kernels
10 cups water
1 cup culinary ash (see note), or
    2 tablespoons baking soda

Soak the dried corn overnight in a bowl filled with the water.

The following day, place the corn and water into an enameled pot. (Culinary ash reacts with metal, so the hominy must be processed in an enameled pot.) Cover and bring to a boil over high heat.

When the water begins to boil, stir in the culinary ash. At this point, the ash will intensify the color of the kernels.

Cover and decrease the heat. Simmer over low heat for about 5½ hours, until the hulls are loose and the corn returns to its original color. Stir occasionally, replenishing with enough water to cover the corn to keep it from drying out and burning on the bottom.

Under cold running water, rub the corn kernels between your fingers to remove the hulls. Discard the hulls. Drain the corn in a colander.

To dry hominy in the traditional manner, spread the cooked and hulled corn on an open-weave basket or screen and place it in full sun, turning the kernels every few hours until completely dry. This method of drying is an ancient practice and is still used among certain tribes today. Alternatively, a more modern method is to place the kernels on a sheet pan in a gas oven with the pilot light on, or in an electric oven on the lowest setting, turning every few hours until dry. To check if the corn is ready, break open a kernel: if there is any moisture inside, keep drying. Once properly dried, hominy will keep for a full year without spoiling.
Makes 5 cups cooked or 3 cups dried hominy

NOTE: Culinary ash is made from burning the wood of certain trees until there is only ash left. Many types of trees and bushes found throughout the Southwest can be used; the Diné (Navajo) use juniper primarily, and the Hopi use green plants such as *suuvi* or *chamisa* bushes. The green twigs, when burned, produce an ash with a high mineral content. When used in cooking, it increases the food's nutritional value.

When culinary ash is mixed with boiling water and corn, the alkali in the ash reacts with the corn and changes it to a more intense color. After the water has cooled, the corn changes back to something close to its original color.

If you are in an area where culinary ash is difficult to obtain (see Source Guide, page 201), baking soda can be used as a substitute, although it doesn't have the high nutritional value of ash.

*Opposite: Indian hominy drying for later use (top).
Richard Mermejo (Picuris Pueblo) with Truchas Peaks
in the background (bottom).*

POSOLE

1½ cups dried Indian Hominy (page 29)

6 quarts water

2 ham hocks (approximately 2 lbs.)

2 dried red New Mexico chiles, seeded, stemmed, and
  torn into 6 pieces

1 small onion, chopped

3 cloves garlic, chopped

1 teaspoon fresh oregano leaves, finely chopped
  (or dried Mexican oregano)

1 teaspoon azafrán (Native American saffron; see note,
  page 125)

Soak the hominy overnight in 1 quart of water.

The following day, drain and discard the water. Place the hominy in a large pot filled with the remaining 5 quarts of water. Bring to a boil over high heat, then decrease heat and simmer for about 4 hours, until the kernels burst and are puffy and tender. (White corn tends to puff the most.)

Add more water, if necessary, to cover the kernels. Add the ham hocks, red chiles, onion, and garlic, and cook for another 1½ hours, until the meat is tender and falling off the bone. Add the oregano and *azafrán* and cook for another 15 minutes.

Remove the meat from the bones and discard the bones. Return the meat to the pot. If you are eating this as a stew by itself you may want to add a little more water. Return to the stove and serve hot.

Makes 3 cups; serves 6

Posole *is a simple, rustic stew common throughout the pueblos of New Mexico. Made from dried hominy corn, ham hocks, spices, and dried red chile, the stew is usually cooked in large quantities. It is customarily eaten on each Pueblo's Feast Day, when the Pueblo's Patron Saint is celebrated, and on New Year's Day, when a hearty meal for cold weather is welcome. The stew is traditionally served with a variety of condiments. It tastes especially good with Red Chile Sauce (page 64), freshly roasted diced green chiles (page 61), chile pequín (a small spicy dried chile), and any of the Indian breads, my favorite being the Adobe Bread (page 68).*

INDIAN TORTILLAS

Tortillas have been made by Native peoples in the Southwest and throughout Mexico for centuries. Making tortillas is considered by some to be an art form in itself. For the novice, it can be time-consuming and a bit difficult, but fresh, warm tortillas make the process worthwhile. Corn masa mixes are available commercially now in supermarkets, which makes the process easier. Tortillas will keep well in the refrigerator for about 5 days when covered in plastic. To reheat, simply warm on an ungreased griddle or open flame.

BLUE CORNMEAL TORTILLAS

2 cups very finely ground blue cornmeal
1 cup flour
2 teaspoons salt
2 teaspoons baking powder
4 tablespoons lard or vegetable shortening
1 cup plus 3 tablespoons water or milk
Cilantro leaves or other fresh herb (optional)

Mix the blue cornmeal, flour, salt, and baking powder together in a bowl. With your hands, work in the lard and 1 cup water or milk until completely mixed and pliable. Gradually mix in the remaining water, 1 tablespoon at a time, to make a stiff dough that is dry enough not to stick to a wooden work surface or tortilla press. You may not need all of the remaining water.

Knead the dough in a bowl for 5 minutes. Pinch off about 1½ tablespoons of dough and roll it into a ball between your palms. Press into a flat circle on the work surface and place a cilantro leaf in the center. Roll the dough out with a rolling pin or place in a tortilla press between two sheets of plastic (I cut a plastic freezer bag for this) and flatten to make round cakes, 6 to 7 inches in diameter and no thicker than ⅛ inch.

Heat a large cast-iron skillet or griddle over medium-high heat. Brown the tortillas, as many as will fit in your skillet or griddle, for about 3 minutes on each side. While the other tortillas are cooking, keep the finished tortillas warm between clean, folded kitchen towels.
Makes about 20 tortillas

NOTE: For a spicy flavor, impressions can be made into the just-cooked tortillas with a shucked corncob dipped in Red Chile Sauce (page 64) or Gaujillo Chile Sauce (page 47).

*Opposite: Blue and yellow cornmeal tortillas (top).
Red, white, and blue Indian corn (bottom).*

YELLOW CORNMEAL TORTILLAS

Yellow corn tortillas are traditionally made from ground dried hominy or from a lime-treated corn mixture called nixtamal. From this a masa is made and used for tortillas. It is a time-consuming process. For greater convenience, masa harina, a basic mix for making this dough, is available in most supermarkets. When using the commercial mix, follow the manufacturer's instructions for making the masa.

2 cups masa (recipe is on facing page) or masa harina
½ teaspoon salt
1⅓ cups warm water

Using your hands or a wooden spoon, mix together the masa and salt in a bowl. Add the water and mix until the dough holds its form. It should be a stiff but pliable dough, still dry enough not to stick to a wooden work surface or tortilla press.

Knead the dough in the bowl for 5 minutes. Pinch off about 1½ tablespoons of dough and roll it into a ball between your palms. Press into a flat circle on the work surface. (As in the Blue Cornmeal Tortillas recipe, page 33, you can add cilantro leaves or other fresh herbs at this point by pressing a leaf into the dough.)

Roll the dough out with a rolling pin or place in a tortilla press between two sheets of plastic (I cut a plastic freezer bag into two pieces for this) and flatten to make round cakes, 6 to 7 inches in diameter and no thicker than ⅛ inch.

Heat a large cast-iron skillet or griddle over medium-high heat. Brown the tortillas, as many as will fit in your skillet or griddle, for about 2 minutes on each side. While the other tortillas are cooking, keep the finished tortillas warm between clean, folded kitchen towels.
Makes 15 to 18 tortillas

FLOUR TORTILLAS

2½ cups flour
1½ teaspoons salt
1 teaspoon baking powder
6 tablespoons lard or vegetable shortening
¾ cup hot water

In a bowl, mix together the flour, salt, and baking powder. Add the lard and thoroughly work it into the dry ingredients.

Place the flour-and-lard mixture on a flat work surface, making a depression in the middle. Pour the water into the well and mix together with your hands. Knead for about 5 minutes until the dough is pliable. The dough should be moist but dry enough not to stick to a work surface or tortilla press. If the dough is sticky, add a little more flour. Put the dough in the refrigerator to rest for 1 hour.

Divide the dough into 10 to 12 pieces of about 1½ tablespoons each and shape them into balls. Roll the dough out with a rolling pin or place in a tortilla press between two sheets of plastic (I cut a plastic freezer bag into two pieces for this) and flatten to make circles, 6 to 7 inches in diameter and no thicker than ⅛ inch thick.

Heat a large cast-iron skillet or griddle over high heat until very hot (flour tortillas taste best when cooked quickly over high heat). Cook each tortilla until it puffs and browns, flip it over, press down with a spatula to get rid of any air bubbles, and brown the other side as well. Wrap the cooked tortillas in a clean kitchen towel to keep warm, or reheat them in the traditional way, over an open flame.
Makes 10 to 12 tortillas

MAKING MASA FROM SCRATCH

Although time consuming, this is the traditional method for making corn masa for tortillas and is still prepared by many Native American cooks.

2 cups cold water
2 cups culinary ash (see note, page 29), or
  ¼ cup baking soda
2 pounds dried yellow corn

In a small glass bowl, mix together the cold water and culinary ash until dissolved.

Place the dried corn in a large enamel or other nonreactive (nonaluminum) pot with water to cover by about 2 inches. Place the pot over low heat, add half of the ash water, and stir well. The skins of the corn kernels should start to turn yellow. Add the remainder of the ash water and stir again.

Bring the corn-ash mixture to a boil over high heat, then decrease the heat and gently simmer for 2 to 3 hours, until you can rub the skins off the corn easily. Stir occasionally to prevent burning, and add more water to cover as necessary. Remove from the heat.

Drain the mixture (known at this stage as *nixtamal*), rinse in cold water, then drain again. With your hands, rub the corn kernels to remove the skins completely. Now the *nixtamal* is ready to be ground into masa. Traditionally, *nixtamal* is ground by hand on a matate (a flat grinding stone used for corn), though it can also be ground in a food processor. I have seen small stores with large corn grinding machines, called *molinos,* in small villages throughout regions of Mexico, where women still take their soaked cooked corn to be ground.

Process the *nixtamal* until completely ground. The coarser the grind, the coarser the tortilla meal will be. The resulting masa will last, covered in the refrigerator, for 5 to 7 days.
Makes 3 cups

NOTE: Prepared masa or nixtamal can be purchased at specialty stores or Latin American markets. Some stores sell masa already mixed frozen in the freezer section.

CHAQUEWA (TESUQUE INDIAN PORRIDGE)

Chaquewa, *a traditional porridge, has been served for centuries by the Native American peoples of the Southwest, usually during the cold months of winter. In the high-altitude regions of northern New Mexico, the winters grow frigid and a hot breakfast helps to warm up a cold morning. It is traditional to serve this porridge with milk, or with sliced fruit if it is available (peaches and strawberries are New Mexican favorites). Sue Dorame at Tesuque Pueblo taught me this recipe.*

2 cups water
2 cups finely ground blue cornmeal
½ teaspoon salt
3 cups milk

In a saucepan, bring the water to a boil over high heat. Add the cornmeal and salt and stir constantly until completely mixed. Decrease the heat to low and continue to stir for about 7 minutes. The porridge will thicken as it cooks. Remove from the heat.

In another saucepan, warm the milk over medium heat. Pour the milk over the porridge and serve warm.
Serves 6

VARIATION: As the boiled cornmeal cools, it hardens to a doughy, breadlike consistency; it is sometimes served as a quick bread. While the mixture is still warm, the women mold it into a loaf shape with their hands. They allow it to cool, then sometimes they reheat it, and cut it into slices.

ATOLE

With a different ratio of water to cornmeal, the same basic ingredients of chaquewa *can also be made into a blue cornmeal drink called* atole, *a warm drink popular among the Pueblos that is usually served in the morning.*

½ cup finely ground blue cornmeal
3¾ cups water
1 teaspoon sugar

Mix the cornmeal and ¾ cup of the water together in a small mixing bowl to make a thin paste. In a saucepan, bring the remaining 3 cups water to a boil over high heat. Add the paste to the boiling water. Stirring constantly, add the sugar and bring the mixture to a full boil. Remove from the heat and continue stirring until the mixture is cool enough to drink. For those who do not like sweet beverages, some Southwest Indian cooks add salt instead of sugar.
Serves 4 to 6

Above: Adobe houses, Taos Pueblo, New Mexico.

BLUE CORNMEAL AND PIÑON HOTCAKES WITH PRICKLY PEAR SYRUP AND PEACH HONEY

This recipe was taught to me as a breakfast dish, but it also makes a wonderful dessert. Try the piñon hotcakes with the Pumpkin Ice Cream (page 97). The piñon hotcakes are dense and nutty, and the blue cornmeal hotcakes light and delicious. They combine perfectly with the prickly pear syrup and peach honey and make for a wonderful weekend breakfast with the family.

PIÑON HOTCAKES
1½ cups piñons (pine nuts)
1 cup flour
½ teaspoon salt
2 tablespoons sugar
1 cup milk

BLUE CORNMEAL HOTCAKES
1½ cups blue cornmeal
2 tablespoons sugar
1 tablespoon baking powder
1 teaspoon salt
3 tablespoons unsalted butter, melted
2 eggs, beaten
1 cup milk

4 tablespoons unsalted butter, melted, for greasing
   the griddle
Prickly Pear Syrup (page 121)
Peach Honey (page 131)

To make the hotcakes, grind the piñons to a coarse meal in a food processor or blender. Mix the ground nut meal together with the flour, salt, and sugar, and add the milk to form a stiff batter. Set aside and let stand for 1 hour before cooking.

To make the blue cornmeal pancakes, in a large bowl, combine the cornmeal, sugar, baking powder, and salt. Add the butter, eggs, and milk, and mix thoroughly.

Warm a griddle over medium heat and lightly brush with some of the melted butter

Drop spoonfuls of the batters onto the griddle. The piñon hotcakes may have to be pressed with a well-greased spatula into ¼- to ½-inch-thick cakes, 3 inches in diameter, because the batter is very thick. Turn the cakes once as they begin to brown. To keep the finished hotcakes warm, stack them on a cookie sheet, cover them with a clean towel, and place them in the oven set at a very low heat. Butter the griddle between each batch of hotcakes.

Above: Cassandra Lyn Begay and Tiffany Georgeina Morgan (Diné) from Pinon, Arizona, harvesting corn in Cassandra's grandfather Thomas Mike's cornfield.

SOMEVIKI WITH RED CHILE SAUCE

Someviki *are sweet blue cornmeal dumplings that are wrapped in corn husks, tied, and boiled until cooked. Many tribes make their own version of this dish, some referring to it as a sweet cornbread that can be eaten with beans, soups, or stews. Here, it is served with red chile sauce. The sweetness of the cornmeal complements the spicy flavor of the red chile sauce very nicely. This is one of my favorite Hopi dishes; Juanita Tiger Kavena, who has written a book entitled* Hopi Cookery, *taught it to me.*

30 dried corn husks
5 tablespoons culinary ash (see note, page 29), or
   2 teaspoons baking soda
2 cups boiling water
2½ cups finely ground blue cornmeal
⅓ cup sugar
Red Chile Sauce (page 64)

Soak the corn husks in very hot water for 10 to 15 minutes, until they are soft and pliable.

Mix the culinary ash with ½ cup of the boiling water in a glass measuring cup and set aside.

Mix the blue cornmeal and sugar together in a bowl. Add the remaining boiling water and stir until the mixture is thick.

Pour the ash water through a very fine strainer; discard the ash. Add the ash water to the cornmeal mixture, small amounts at a time, while stirring to make the dough. It will turn a distinctive blue color and should have the consistency of a thick cake batter. If it is too thin, you will need to add a little more blue cornmeal.

Spoon 1 tablespoon of the dough onto each corn husk and fold the husk around the dough, first the sides and then the ends. Tear long, thin strands from another husk and tie each bundle to secure the dough inside. You may have to use 2 corn husk ties around each bundle to secure them.

Bring a large pot of water to a boil, drop the wrapped husks into the water, and simmer for 12 to 15 minutes. Once the husks have plumped, remove them from the water and drain. Serve with the corn husks on so that the dumplings stay hot; diners can untie and discard the husks. Serve with the chile sauce.

Makes approximately 30 someviki, serves 8 to 10 as an appetizer

NOTE: Those at higher altitudes will need to add 1 minute of cooking time for every 1,000 feet of altitude.

Above: Jolene Eustace-Hanelt (Zuni and Cochiti Pueblo) in a traditional manta.

SPICY CORN SOUP

There is nothing like the taste of fresh sweet corn. I usually make this soup during the summer months, when corn is at its sweetest, but it can be made at any time of the year. Its spicy flavor comes from chipotle chile powder. Jalapeños that have been dried and then smoked are referred to as chipotles. Dried chipotle chiles can be ground into a powder and used for seasoning. This medium-size, thick fleshed chile is smoky and sweet and has a subtle, deep, rounded heat. In Santa Fe, local farmers sell fresh ground chipotle chile powder, but it is also available by mail order (see Source Guide, page 201).

4 ears of corn, or 3 cups corn kernels (fresh, frozen, or
   canned)
1 tablespoon olive oil
1 yellow onion, diced
1 tablespoon garlic, finely chopped (about 5 cloves)
1 tablespoon dried chipotle chile powder
1 teaspoon salt
½ teaspoon black pepper
6 cups chicken stock (page 198)
1 red bell pepper
1½ cups heavy cream

Prepare the corn by cutting the kernels from the cob. You should have about 3 cups of kernels from 4 cobs of corn. Save the corn cobs and set aside. The cobs will add additional corn flavor to the soup.

In a saucepan over medium-high heat, add the oil, then the onion. Sauté for 3 to 4 minutes, stirring occasionally, until the onion is translucent. Add the garlic and chipotle chile powder and sauté for 1 more minute. Add the corn kernels and sauté for another 3 minutes, stirring constantly.

Add the salt, black pepper, and stock and bring to a boil. (If you have cut your corn fresh from the cob, place the reserved cobs into the saucepan at this time.) Once the mixture reaches a boil, decrease the heat and simmer for 30 minutes. Stir occasionally to prevent the corn kernels from burning or sticking to the bottom of the pan.

While the soup is simmering, roast the red bell pepper using the open flame method (page 61), then peel, seed, and dice it. Place the diced bell pepper into a blender with ½ cup of the heavy cream and blend thoroughly for 1 minute. Pour through a fine sieve and discard the contents of the sieve. Pour the red bell pepper sauce into a plastic squirt bottle and set aside.

Remove the corn soup mixture from the heat and discard the corn cobs. Place the corn soup mixture in a blender and purée for 3 minutes. Pour the mixture through a sieve and discard the contents of the sieve.

Return the mixture to a saucepan, add the remaining 1 cup of heavy cream, and heat over medium heat for 15 minutes, stirring occasionally to prevent burning. Pour into bowls, garnish with some of the red pepper sauce, and serve immediately.

Serves 6

Above: Mara Fiona Selestewa (Hopi/Diné) with an ear of fresh blue Indian corn.

Traditionally, cornsicles are made with either fresh yellow or blue corn alone; the sweet, fresh taste of the corn needs no embellishment. Here, we've presented the recipe with the addition of shrimp and oregano, which enhance the flavor of the sweet corn. Try serving them as appetizers or as an accompaniment to an entrée.

6 ears fresh corn
18 fresh corn husk leaves or dried soaked corn husks
1 teaspoon salt
¼ teaspoon white pepper
1 tablespoon chopped fresh oregano, or 1 teaspoon dried
12 medium shrimp, peeled, deveined, and diced

18 popsicle sticks

Trim the corn and remove the husks and silk. Wash and save the larger fresh corn husks. (If using dried corn husks, soak them in warm water for about 10 minutes to make them more pliable.) Cut the corn kernels from the cob, scraping out as much milk as you can. (The corn milk is what binds the cornsicles together.)

Grind the kernels using a food processor or a meat grinder with a sharp blade. If using a food processor, make sure to stir the corn well with a spatula so that all of the corn kernels have been ground. Add the salt, pepper, oregano, and shrimp and process for another 10 to 15 seconds.

Preheat the oven to 325°.

Drop a tablespoon of the corn mixture onto the center of a clean husk. Fold the left side of the husk into the center, then the right, and then fold the bottom end upward. (This folding process is very similar to that of making a tamale.) Push a popsicle stick 2 to 3 inches into the open end and pinch the husk around the stick with your fingers. Tear a thin strand from a dry husk and tie it around the cornsicle. You can use some of the smaller husks to make ties for the other cornsicles.

Place the cornsicles, standing upright with the sticks in the air and very close together, in a glass baking dish 5 by 9 inches or a loaf pan the same size. Bake for 30 minutes, until the corn mixture is firm and solid.

To eat a cornsicle, peel off the corn husk and eat it hot from the stick. Serve these with either the fresh Green Chile Sauce (page 65) or the Indian Salsa (page 76).

Makes about 18; serves 6 as an appetizer

BLUE CORN GNOCCHI ARROWHEADS WITH GUAJILLO CHILE SAUCE

In this dish, I have used blue cornmeal, a standard ingredient in Native American Southwest cooking, to make a dumpling very similar to gnocchi, a classic Italian potato dumpling. The cornmeal makes the dough thicker and more pliable, which makes cutting the dumplings into interesting shapes easy. Here, I have shaped the dumplings into arrowheads, but you can make them round, oblong, or rectangular.

BLUE CORN GNOCCHI

2 medium russet potatoes, peeled
8 quarts water
5 ounces (about ½ cup) soft white goat cheese
4 eggs
1½ cups all-purpose flour
1½ cups finely ground blue cornmeal
2 tablespoons salt

GUAJILLO CHILE SAUCE

3 ounces dried guajillo chiles (about 15 chiles or 2¼ cups)
½ cup dried pumpkin seeds
⅓ teaspoon salt
½ teaspoon white pepper
2½ cups water
3 cups chicken stock (page 198)

To make the gnocchi, boil the potatoes in 2 quarts of the water until they are soft and cooked through, approximately 10 minutes.

In a food processor, combine the potatoes and goat cheese and process until free of lumps, about 2 minutes. Add the eggs and process for another minute. The mixture should resemble putty.

In a separate mixing bowl, stir the flour and blue cornmeal together. Pour the potato mixture into another mixing bowl and add 2 cups of the flour-cornmeal mixture. Mix together thoroughly to form the dough.

Dust a wooden cutting board with half of the remaining flour-cornmeal mixture and place the dough on top. Flatten it and sprinkle it with the remaining flour-cornmeal mixture. Knead the flour-cornmeal mixture into the dough until it becomes stiff. The dough is ready when it no longer clings to the board. If the mixture is still soft, damp, and sticky, knead in a little more flour.

With your hands, shape the dough on a board into a long roll 2 inches in diameter. With a knife cut the dough into 1-inch-thick slices.

Flour another board and roll each 1-inch piece into a thin strip about ½ inch wide and 16 inches long. Flatten the strips with your hands to about 1 inch wide, and cut the dough with a knife or cookie cutter into arrowheads or any other shape you desire. Set aside. (I usually put the gnocchi on a cookie sheet lined with parchment paper that has been dusted with flour so they don't stick. They can be made ahead of time and placed on the cookie sheet until they are ready to be cooked.)

To make the chile sauce, stem and remove the seeds from the guajillo chiles. Place the chiles, pumpkin seeds, salt, and pepper in a food processor and process for 1 minute. Add the water in small amounts until completely blended, about 4 minutes. Press the mixture through a fine sieve and discard the contents of the sieve.

In a saucepan, add the stock and the chile mixture and heat over medium-high heat for 4 minutes, until it begins to boil. Decrease the heat and simmer for 15 to 20 minutes, until thickened. The sauce should reduce by about half.

While the sauce is simmering, cook the gnocchi. In a large pot, bring the remaining 6 quarts water to a boil with the salt. Add the gnocchi and cook for 2 to 3 minutes (see note), gently stirring frequently so that they don't stick. At first the gnocchi will sink to the bottom; as they cook, they will begin to hold their shape and float to the surface.

Once the gnocchi have risen to the top, remove them from the boiling water with a slotted spoon.

Spoon ½ cup of sauce onto each plate, top with the gnocchi, and serve immediately.
Serves 6 as an appetizer

NOTE: At higher altitudes, gnocchi can take longer to cook. Usually, I allow 1 extra minute of cooking for each 1,000 feet of altitude. Always test before serving.

Hazruquive (Hominy, Bean Sprout, and Corncob Stew)

This recipe is based on a traditional Hopi dish made once a year on the day of the Powamu Ceremony, or Bean Dance, in late winter. It celebrates the changing of the seasons. I have adapted this recipe using fresh corn cobs because dried corn on the cob is not readily available commercially. For those of you who wish to make this recipe the traditional way using dried corn on the cob, double the number of corn cobs and cook them overnight until they are tender, then follow the recipe as I have written it.

2 cups cooked Indian Hominy (page 29) or
    Posole (page 31)
3 cups veal stock (page 200)
1 teaspoon salt
½ teaspoon black pepper
3 ears yellow corn on the cob, cut into 3- to
    4-inch pieces
2 bunches (about 3 ounces) bean or sunflower sprouts

Place the hominy in a large saucepan with enough water to cover. Bring to a boil over high heat and add the veal stock, salt, and pepper. Return to a boil, decrease the heat to medium, and cook for 10 to 15 minutes.

Add the corn and continue cooking for about 10 minutes longer, or until the corn is tender.

Add the bean sprouts, decrease the heat to low, and simmer until they also are tender, 5 to 10 minutes.

Serve hot. *Hazruquive* tastes wonderful with *Piki Bread* (page 51) or any of the other Indian breads.
Serves 6

Chicos and Lamb Stew

In New Mexico, small dried kernels of corn that have been roasted in an outdoor adobe oven are called chicos. This recipe is a traditional stew primarily prepared throughout New Mexico.

1 pound *chicos* (see Source Guide, page 201)
10 cups water
1 tablespoon olive oil
1 yellow onion, diced
1 tablespoon garlic, finely chopped (about 5 cloves)
1 pound lamb stew meat, cut into 1-inch cubes
4 green New Mexico or Anaheim chiles
1 teaspoon salt
½ teaspoon black pepper

Place the *chicos* in a large saucepot, add the water, and bring to a boil. Decrease the heat and simmer for 2½ hours. In a skillet, heat the olive oil over medium-high heat. Add the onion and sauté for 4 minutes until translucent. Add the garlic and sauté for 30 seconds; add the meat and sauté for 4 minutes until brown, about 2 minutes on each side. Remove from the heat.

Add the sautéed meat to the *chicos* and stir. Bring to a boil, then decrease the heat and simmer for 1 hour.

Roast the green chiles using the open flame method (page 61), then peel, seed, devein, and chop them. After the meat and *chicos* have cooked for 1 hour, add the chopped green chiles, salt, and black pepper, and simmer for an additional 15 minutes. Serve immediately with one of the Indian breads from this book.
Serves 6 to 8

PIKI BREAD

Piki is a paper-thin cornbread and is considered one of the original Indian breads. *Piki* is of Hopi origin, but it is made in many of the Pueblos. Each Pueblo that makes this bread has its own name for it, but essentially it is the same bread. It is a blue cornmeal batter that is baked in large tissue-paper–thin sheets and then rolled up like a newspaper. Occasionally, white, yellow, or pink *piki* is made for special dances. The making of *piki* is an art and a ritual, and it takes years of practice to become a good *piki* maker. In the past, a young woman was required to demonstrate that she had mastered the art of making *piki* before she could be considered a suitable bride. Today, there are fewer women mastering the art of making *piki,* but women still make this paper-thin cornbread.

Piki is traditionally made on a *piki* stone that has been placed in a special little house called the *piki* house. The stone is a large, flat, smooth stone that is approximately 4 to 6 inches thick by 24 to 28 inches long and about 18 inches wide. The stone is usually elevated—raised on four legs so that pieces of wood, usually cedar, can be burned underneath to heat the stone. A small fire is kept burning the entire time *piki* is being made. *Piki* stones take a long time to prepare and are heirlooms that have been handed down for generations from mother to daughter. They are usually kept greased. They are greased with watermelon seeds by some women and bone marrow or cooked brains by others.

The *piki* batter is usually prepared with just three ingredients: a very finely ground blue cornmeal, culinary ash, and water. The *piki* maker dips her hand in the batter and then rubs it onto the hot stone, continuing to add strokes of batter until it forms a large sheet almost the size of the stone. This thin dough is then cooked until it dries and then is pulled off in one large sheet. Another *piki* is then laid down onto the stone and the previous sheet placed on top, until it softens. It is folded several times, and then rolled, resulting in a rolled bread about the size of an ear of corn.

I watched Genevieve Kaursgowva, from Hotevilla, Arizona, on the Hopi reservation make *piki* in her *piki* house and was amazed at how effortless she made it look. When I tried it, the batter globbed in one area of the stone and I burned my hand as it stuck to the hot stone. We laughed and I tried again, with not much more luck than the first attempt. Learning to make *piki* takes time and patience. The trick is to get just enough batter on your fingers and then glide your "battered" fingers over the face of the stone with the thinnest layer of batter separating your fingers from the burning surface.

PIKI BREAD

This recipe is adapted, with permission, from Hopi Cookery by Juanita Tiger Kavena, University of Arizona Press. If you don't have access to a piki stone, this recipe will also work on a greased cast iron griddle.

3 tablespoons culinary ash (see note, page 29)
6½ to 8½ cups cold water
6 cups finely ground blue cornmeal
8 cups boiling water

In a small, non-aluminum bowl, mix the culinary ash with ½ cup of the cold water and set aside.

Put 4 cups of the cornmeal into a large shallow bowl. Pour half of the boiling water over the cornmeal and stir with a wooden spoon until well blended. Gradually add the remaining boiling water, stirring to make a heavy, stiff dough.

Slowly strain the ash water through a cheesecloth-lined sieve into the dough, stirring to blend.

When the dough is cool enough to handle, knead it by hand until smooth and all the lumps are dissolved. Work in the remaining cornmeal, small amounts at a time. Set the dough aside to rest about 10 minutes and build a fire under the piki stone.

While the stone is heating, gradually add the remaining cold water a little at a time into the dough, adding enough to make a smooth, thin batter no thicker

than cream. As you cook the piki, you may find it necessary to add more cold water, as the batter tends to thicken.

Grease the hot stone. You may need to regrease the stone after every two or three piki.

Dip your hand into the batter and spread the batter across the stone, moving from left to right and back again, touching the stone lightly with your fingers. Dip your fingers back into the batter and continue spreading the batter across the stone, overlapping the previous strip, until the stone is completely covered.

When the piki is done, the edges will separate from the stone. Gently lift it off with your hands and place it on a piki tray, a basket that is used to hold piki. (The first piece of piki is traditionally "fed to the fire" and the stone is asked at this time "to work well and not be lazy" for the cook.)

Spread more batter on the stone. As soon as the surface is dry, place the already-cooked piki on top and let it soften. Warming the paper-thin piki will prevent it from cracking easily. Fold two opposite sides of the warm piki a quarter of the way toward the center, then gently roll the piki and move it to the tray. Lift the next piki from the stone as it is done and repeat the process.

Continue the procedure with the remaining batter until all the batter has been used.
Makes about 50 piki

Above: Genevieve Kaursgouvva (Hopi) from Hotevilla, Arizona, making blue corn piki bread on a piki stone. Right: Stacks of freshly made yellow piki bread.

BLUE CORNBREAD

Blue cornbread can be served with soups or stews, for breakfast with any of the fruit sauces and jellies described in this book, or with a meal as you would any other bread. I like it warm, right out of the oven with melted butter on it.

1 cup blue cornmeal
1 cup flour
3 tablespoons sugar
2 teaspoons baking powder
½ teaspoon baking soda
½ teaspoon salt
2 eggs
1¾ cups buttermilk
2 tablespoons unsalted butter, melted

Preheat the oven to 425°. Grease a 9 by 13-inch baking pan, two corn stick pans, or an 8-inch cast-iron skillet.

In a large bowl, mix together the cornmeal, flour, sugar, baking powder, baking soda, and salt.

In a separate bowl, mix together the eggs and buttermilk. Gradually stir the wet ingredients into the dry ingredients. Mix well. Then add the melted butter and stir again. Do not overstir the mixture.

Spoon the batter into the prepared pan(s) and bake until firm, 25 to 30 minutes if using a baking pan or skillet or 15 to 20 minutes if using corn stick pans. The bread should be golden brown and spring back when touched. *Makes 1 pan of cornbread or 14 corn sticks*

POSOLE TERRINE WITH AZAFRÁN SAUCE

The three subtle colors of corn—red, white, and blue—meld together in one terrine, creating a beautiful dish. It has a rich, sweet corn flavor that is very delicious. The terrine can be eaten alone or served, as presented here, with azafrán *sauce as an appetizer or an entrée.*

POSOLE TERRINE

2½ cups cooked red hominy or posole
  (pages 29 and 31)
2½ cups cooked white hominy or posole
  (pages 29 and 31)
2½ cups cooked blue hominy or posole
  (pages 29 and 31)
6 eggs
1½ teaspoons salt
¾ teaspoon white pepper
4½ cups heavy cream
3 egg whites

AZAFRÁN SAUCE

1 shallot, coarsely chopped
2 cloves garlic, finely chopped
1 tablespoon olive oil
1 cup chicken stock (page 198)

3 cups heavy cream
4 tablespoons *azafrán* (see note, page 125)
½ teaspoon salt
½ teaspoon white pepper

To make the terrine, in a food processor, blend each cooked hominy separately for 2 to 3 minutes, until smooth. Add 2 eggs, ½ teaspoon salt, and ¼ teaspoon pepper to each batch of hominy and process again for 2 minutes. Adding small amounts at a time, slowly pulse in 1½ cups of the cream and then 1 egg white into each batch of hominy. Do this slowly, so as not to curdle the cream while pulsing. Press through a fine sieve to remove the skins and any lumps. Set aside.

Preheat the oven to 350°.

Fill a buttered, 5 by 9-inch glass loaf pan one-third full with one layer of the corn purée. Pour a second corn purée layer (of another color) and top with the remaining purée. Tap the terrine on the table to level the purées and then cover with parchment paper.

Place the baking dish in a roasting pan. Add water to the pan reaching two-thirds of the way up the loaf pan. Bake for 1 hour, until firm throughout. Remove from the oven and allow to cool and set. The terrine will keep, covered, in the refrigerator for up to 5 days.

To make the sauce, sauté the shallot and garlic in olive oil in a saucepan over high heat for 2 minutes. Add the stock, decrease the heat to medium, and reduce the mixture by half, about 5 minutes. Remove from the heat and strain, discarding the shallot and garlic.

Return the mixture to the saucepan and add the cream and *azafrán*. Continue to simmer over medium heat until the mixture has reduced by half again, about 5 minutes. Add the salt and pepper and stir well.

Meanwhile, to reheat the terrine, cut it into slices and place the slices about ½ inch apart on a large cookie sheet lined with parchment paper. Place another piece of parchment paper over the top and bake in a preheated 400° oven for about 10 minutes, or until hot.

Spoon some of the sauce onto individual plates and serve with the terrine.

Serves 10 to 12 as an appetizer or 8 as a main course

CORN AND HONEY ICE

Walter Whitewater remembers his grandmother making this dessert when he was a child. She would cook blue or red cornmeal, placing it outside when it was cold out, and all the grandchildren would eat the corn ice in the morning when it had frozen. The pastel colors in this ice are achieved by using dried red or blue cornmeal. You can also use fresh white corn and add 2 tablespoons blue cornmeal to the saucepan for the blue ice or a few fresh raspberries or strawberries for the red.

3 cups fresh corn kernels
1 tablespoon vegetable oil
1 cup water
⅓ cup honey

Place the corn and oil in a saucepan and cook over medium heat for 4 minutes, stirring constantly to prevent the corn from browning. Transfer the corn to a blender and add the water and honey. Blend until very smooth.

Return the mixture to the saucepan and bring to a boil. Decrease the heat and simmer, uncovered, stirring frequently, about 15 minutes, until it has a thick, porridgelike consistency.

Freeze for at least 6 hours or place in an ice cream maker and follow the manufacturer's directions.
Serves 6

Above: Strands of freshly harvested corn drying for winter use.

CHILES
THE SPICE OF LIFE

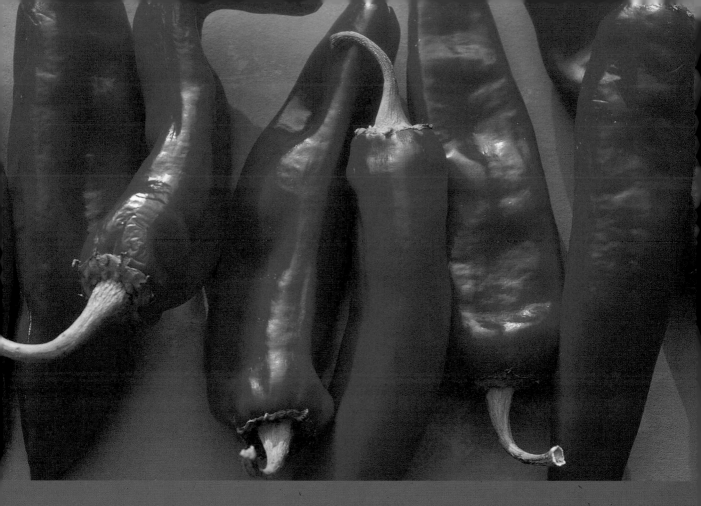

BY THE TIME Europeans arrived in the New World, peppers had migrated from South America into Mesoamerica and the Caribbean, and all five of the domesticated forms that are now recognized had been developed. This fruit, which grows on plants of the genus *Capsicum*, is a member of the Solanaceae family as are the tomato and potato.

There were three species of cultivated chiles in ancient America. The most aberrant is the *Capsicum pubescens*. This species is unique because it has a great tolerance for cold and has purple flowers, dark seeds, and slightly fuzzy leaves and stems. *Capsicum pubescens* was probably first domesticated in the highlands of Bolivia, later spreading into the highlands of Peru.[i] The taste of these chiles is quite different from the pungent chiles we are familiar with today.

The white-flowered and white-seeded *Capsicum annuum*, *Capsicum chinense*, and *Caspsicum frutescens*

species originated in tropical South America. *Capsicum annuum*, however, was found wild, in the Tehuacan Valley dating from 7200 to 5200 B.C.[ii] *Capsicum frutescens* produces the chile that is used to make Tabasco sauce, and *Capsicum chinense* includes the Scotch bonnet and habanero chile. However, it is the *Capsicum annuum* that gives us most of the chiles we know today.

The third species, *Capsicum baccatum*, also a white-seeded chile, has brown or yellow spots at the base of its white flower petals. It is primarily used in tropical South America and is distinguishable by its shape and appearance.

When Columbus arrived, he found a New World treasure widely used by the Natives in the Americas and on the islands of the Caribbean. This pungent flavoring was a fruit referred to as *ají* by the Natives living there. Columbus called this unfamiliar spice "pepper" or *pimiento* after the black pepper *pimienta*, which he had been seeking. He carried specimens of this new pepper (which actually belonged to the genus *Capsicum* and not to *Piper nigrum)* back to the Iberian Peninsula, and from there it spread rapidly around the globe, changing and enhancing the cuisine of every land it touched. Today it may be the most widely used spice in the world.[iii]

The pungent red fruits of wild chile peppers such as the chiltecpin are erect, easily separated from the stalk when ripe. They were small enough for birds to swallow them and carry the ingested seeds for considerable distances before dropping them, thus establishing the peppers in other regions. Many domesticated forms of chiles also had small fruits. These fruits dried well, making them easy to transport, and they had seeds that remained viable for long periods and could still be germinated once planted in another region or habitat.

Later, when the Spaniards arrived in Mexico, they heard the *ají* that they had seen in the Caribbean and South America being called *chilli,* a Nahuatl word meaning "red," or "red plant." The Spanish changed its name to *chile,* and the name of this spicy fruit has stuck ever since. Today, the term *chile* refers to both hot and sweet types of peppers and green chiles, as well as red.

As chiles migrated northward with the Spanish colonists, they were introduced into the Pueblos along with other foods brought by the Spanish. Because of the climate in the Southwest and the farming techniques that were already in use by the Native Peoples here, especially on the Pueblos, chiles became a part of the cuisine in this region. They began to be cultivated in addition to the corn, beans, and squash that were already being cultivated at the time.[iv]

Ironically, except for the early Spanish colonies in the Southwest, chiles were nowhere to be found north of modern-day Mexico until after colonization by northern Europeans. North America was slow to use these pungent fruits until sometime early in the seventeenth century.[v]

Chiles come in nearly all colors, shapes, sizes, and degrees of pungency. The same plant may have many common names, depending on where the chile plant is grown. Chiles provide vitamins A and C and in small quantities, they aid digestion; but what makes chiles unique is capsaicin. Capsaicin is colorless, odorless, and tasteless. It is, however, a powerful irritant, which is produced by glands where the chile's seed-bearing part, the placenta, meets the wall of the chile fruit. Cooks have for years recommended removing the placenta (or vein, as I call it) and the seeds for a milder taste. Water will not wash off the heat or pungency of a chile, as capsaicin is not soluble in water. There are many tales of how to get rid of the capsaicin once it has penetrated your tongue and mouth, but I haven't found a remedy that is sure to work. The heat in a chile will even vary from plant to plant, so it is difficult for farmers and manufacturers to guarantee a mild or hot product without tasting the crop first. A friend of mine, Jolene Eustace-Hanelt from Cochiti and Zuni Pueblo, told me a story that her oldest sister shared with her. In their family, they never cook with chiles when they are angry because it makes the chiles even hotter.

The most commonly used chiles here in the Southwest are the New Mexico green, (harvested in its unripened state) and the New Mexico red, which is often harvested and then dried in strands commonly called *ristras* and has become an icon of the Southwest itself. The jalapeño is almost always harvested green, and the chipotle is a jalapeño that has been smoked and then dried. The serrano, cayenne, guajillo, chile de árbol, and chile pequín (also called chiltecpin) chiles are also widely used today throughout the Southwest.

Chiles have been a part of the Southwestern diet for hundreds of years and are closely identified with the food of this region today. They are used regularly in many traditional and contemporary dishes and are revered by the people who use them. In the United States, or at least in the Southwest, chiles are truly the spice of life.

CHOOSING AND COOKING WITH CHILES

There are many types of chiles, ranging from mild to fiery hot. The degree of heat depends on the time of harvest and where the chiles were grown. Red chiles are riper than green and usually taste sweeter and less hot as a rule, but there are exceptions. The variety, the growing, and the handling techniques used will also affect the taste and heat of chiles.

The most commonly used chile is the *Anaheim* green chile. It is fairly large—6 to 7 inches long—with mild heat. Harvested green, it is a favorite for stuffing or for roasting and using in sauces and stews. When harvested red, the Anaheim is strung in *ristras,* large strands of chiles that are hung outside in the sun to dry. It can be ground into chile powder once it has completely dried.

The *New Mexico green* chile is similar to the Anaheim, and the two are interchangeable in my recipes. You should note, however, that the New Mexico chile tends to be hotter. It has a flavor unlike that of any other chile in North America: sweet and earthy. The New Mexico green is slightly smaller than the Anaheim and varies in strength from medium to very hot, depending on the region it was grown in. I have found that the chiles grown in the southern part of New Mexico are less hot than the chiles grown in northern New Mexico. They are available fresh almost year-round, although anyone who has been to Santa Fe in the fall knows that these chiles are roasted in huge quantities at that time of the year, when the chile crop has come in. These chiles freeze well, and frozen New Mexico green chiles are better than canned. The *New Mexico red* chile is a ripened New Mexico green. It can be used fresh, but it is more commonly dried and strung into *ristras* or powdered.

The *jalapeño,* about 3 inches long, has a fiery hot taste and, although usually eaten green, can be matured on the vine and ripened to red. It is added raw to salsas and salads or cooked in sauces, soups, and stews. Jalapeños that are roasted, smoked, and then dried are called *chipotles.*

The *serrano,* a smaller chile, can be substituted for the jalapeño. It has a hot but fruity flavor when eaten green; the red pods can be dried, but this chile tastes best when eaten fresh.

The *cayenne* pepper is about 4 to 7 inches in length, and $1/4$ to $3/4$ inch wide. It is a very hot chile with an acidic tart flavor and has a thin flesh tending to twist as it grows; it has the best flavor when it is red and mature, but it is also eaten green.

The *Holland* chile is a hybrid that is available all year and tastes very similar to a fresh cayenne pepper.

The *guajillo* chile is a tough-skinned, dried, brownish-red chile about 4 to 6 inches in length and 1 to 1½ inches wide. It has a rich, earthy flavor that is fruity with a medium hotness.

Other chiles that are eaten dried include the *chile de árbol,* which is usually powdered and almost only used dried, and quite hot. Another extremely hot dried chile is the *chile pequín*. This chile has a light, sweet, smoky flavor but a deep, fiery, transient heat. Both chiles should be used sparingly.

HANDLING CHILES

Always wash fresh and dried chiles to remove dirt. Whenever handling chiles, always take precautions to avoid skin irritation: wear rubber gloves if you are sensitive to chiles and *do not* rub your eyes.

ROASTING CHILES

There are various techniques for roasting chiles, each resulting in a slightly different flavor. Green, red, orange, and yellow bell peppers can be roasted using the same methods.

NOTE: Whichever method you use, once prepared, the chiles can be stored in plastic bags in the refrigerator for up to 1 week, or frozen and kept for up to 6 months.

THE OPEN FLAME METHOD

Roast the whole fresh chiles over a barbecue grill or on a gas stove with the flame set at medium-high. A handy tool to use when roasting chiles on your stove top, is an *asador*. It is an apparatus that fits over your gas or electric burner and has a wire mesh that the chiles can rest on when roasting. These are available at specialty cooking stores. Turn the chiles with tongs every couple of minutes until all parts of the chiles are thoroughly charred.

Remove the chiles from the flame and soak them in ice water or place in a plastic bag to allow them to sweat. Under cold running water, rub the charred skins off and discard.

This method is a better one to use than the oven method (see following page) when you are making stuffed chiles because the meat or flesh of the chile remains firm inside. If using a chile for stuffing or for cooking whole, leave on the stem and make only one slit to remove the veins and seeds, stuff the chile, and reseal it. During chile harvest season, large wire mesh drums are turned over an open flame and chiles are roasted by the bushel. In New Mexico, you can buy roasted chiles, which can be frozen in plastic freezer bags for use throughout the remainder of the year. For those of you in other parts of the country, you can buy frozen roasted chiles that have been peeled, seeded, and chopped. Check your grocer for what is available in your area.

THE OVEN METHOD

Preheat the oven to 450°. Place the chiles on a baking sheet and bake 20 to 30 minutes. Turn the chiles frequently as they begin to brown until all sides are evenly blistered and browned. Remove from the oven.

Sweat the chiles in a closed paper or plastic bag for 5 to 10 minutes, until they are cool enough to handle. Peel each chile and discard the skins. If you are drying the chiles, leave them whole at this point and continue with the drying process. Otherwise, pull off the stems, remove the seeds and veins, and rinse in water to remove any stray seeds. Green chiles are also dried, especially on some of the Pueblos of New Mexico, where they are used whole or ground into a powder for later use.

THE FRYING METHOD

Pour 1 inch of vegetable oil into a saucepan with sides high enough to protect you from spatters. Heat until hot but not quite smoking, then gently drop in enough chiles to cover the bottom of the pan. Turn with tongs as they begin to blister. The skins will loosen as the chiles turn golden brown. Remove from the oil and drain on paper towels. When the chiles are cool enough to handle, peel the skins and discard them. Slice the chiles lengthwise, remove the seeds, devein, remove the stems, and then rinse.

DRYING CHILES

Green chiles can also be dried for future use. Roast and peel the green chiles using the oven method (above). Hang the chiles on a long string or lay them flat on a screen and place outdoors for about 4 days (the weather must be warm and dry). Turn the chiles each day to make sure each side dries equally. Once the chiles are fully dried, they can be bagged and stored in a cool, dry place or ground into a powder.

To reconstitute the dried chiles, soak them in warm water for 1/2 hour, then remove the stems and seeds. The chiles will expand to their original size and can be used as you would fresh chiles. This green chile–drying technique was taught to me and my sister by some of the women at Isleta Pueblo.

For further reading on chiles, check out *The Great Chile Book* by Mark Miller, published by Ten Speed Press.

Opposite: Lupita S. Garcia, Juanita K. Jojola, Teddy Lente, and Anita S. Abeita (Isleta Pueblo, New Mexico).

RED CHILE SAUCE

Once summer is over, brilliant red chiles are hung in strands called ristras *to dry outside many of the adobe houses in the Pueblos of New Mexico and northern Arizona. These* ristras *are strung together after the chiles turn red on the vine and are dried for later use. Used whole or ground in many dishes, these chiles are also made into traditional regional sauces, like this one. Red chile sauce is found at almost every meal on the southwestern Native American table. I like my sauces quite thick so I tend to add less stock, but many cooks here in New Mexico like their sauces a little thinner than I do, adding all 3 cups of stock.*

36 medium dried red New Mexico or Anaheim chiles
   (about 6 cups), rinsed, stemmed, and seeded
1 tablespoon olive oil
2 tablespoons chopped fresh garlic
1 teaspoon salt
2 to 3 cups chicken stock (page 198)
   or rabbit stock (page 199)

Place the chiles in a pot filled with water. Cover, bring to a boil over medium-high heat, then decrease the heat and simmer for 20 to 30 minutes, until the chiles are soft and pliable. Drain the cooked chiles and set aside.

In a small saucepan, heat the oil over medium heat and sauté the garlic for about 2 minutes, until golden brown. Do not burn the garlic as this affects the taste of the sauce.

Place the cooked chiles and the sautéed garlic and the salt into a blender or food processor. Blend to a thick purée. Add the stock in small amounts and continue to blend until the desired consistency is reached. Blend for another minute. Press the sauce through a fine sieve and serve. This sauce can be made ahead of time and will last for about a week in a sealed container in the refrigerator.
Makes about 4 cups

RED CHILE SAUCE #2

This red chile sauce is made from powdered New Mexico or Anaheim red chiles instead of from the dried red chile pods. Sauce from powdered red chiles has a slightly different flavor than other red chile sauces and is used a lot by Indian cooks. You can buy red chile powders that are mild, medium, or hot. I recommend that you try mild or medium until your palate becomes accustomed to the heat of the chiles from the Southwest, and then try the hotter powders.

1 tablespoon olive oil
1 tablespoon garlic, finely chopped
2 cups New Mexico or Anaheim red chile powder
4 cups chicken stock (page 198)
1 teaspoon salt

Heat the oil in a skillet over medium heat until hot but not smoking. Add the garlic and sauté for 1 minute, stirring constantly. Add the red chile powder and stir constantly for 2 more minutes. This process cooks the red chile powder, giving it a nicer flavor.

Add the chicken stock and continue stirring until there are no more lumps left in the sauce. Decrease the heat to low, add the salt, and simmer for 10 minutes, until the sauce has reduced and thickened.
Makes about 5 cups

GREEN CHILE SAUCE

This sauce is an accompaniment to many Southwest dishes and is used in almost every Native American household. It is one of the staple dishes, very similar to Red Chile Sauce (opposite page). Many women make large batches of this sauce and freeze it for later use. In some parts of the Southwest, you can buy containers of frozen green chiles that have already been roasted, peeled, and chopped, which makes this recipe quick and easy to make.

8 green New Mexico or Anaheim chiles
1½ cups chicken stock (page 198)
2 teaspoons chopped fresh garlic
½ teaspoon salt

Using the open flame method (page 61), roast the chiles, then place in a plastic bag or covered bowl and allow them to sweat for several minutes. Stem, seed, and remove the skins from the chiles using cold water. Place the chiles in a blender or food processor with the stock, garlic, and salt. Blend to a thick purée. Press through a fine sieve and serve. This sauce will last for at least a week in a covered container in the refrigerator.
Makes about 2 cups

NOTE: Green chiles will vary in flavor and heat, depending on where they are grown. I have found that northern New Mexico green chiles tend to be smaller and hotter than the chiles grown in the southern portion of the state and those grown in California. You can usually buy them in mild, medium, or hot. Use chiles suitable to your own palate when making this sauce.

FRESH GREEN CHILE SOUP WITH TUMBLEWEED GREENS

Green chiles are found in almost every Southwest kitchen. They are used as a condiment by Native Americans in northern Arizona and throughout the Pueblos in New Mexico. Here, they are used as a base for a spicy and delicious soup. The garnish of tumbleweed greens and sour cream is a refreshingly cool contrast to the fiery taste of the chiles. This dish can be served as a meal in itself with Indian Frybread or Adobe Bread (page 68). It also makes an excellent first course.

12 green New Mexico or Anaheim chiles (see note)
2 medium red bell peppers
2 very large russet potatoes, peeled and cut into
    ½-inch cubes
1½ teaspoons salt
6 cups chicken stock (page 198)
½ teaspoon black pepper
3 cloves garlic, finely chopped
6 tablespoons sour cream, for garnish
½ cup tumbleweed greens or fresh pea sprouts,
    for garnish
1 lime, cut into 6 wedges, for garnish

Roast the chiles and red bell peppers by the open flame method (page 61). Peel the chiles and peppers, pull off the stems, remove the seeds and veins, and set aside.

In a medium saucepan, parboil the potatoes in boiling water with 1 teaspoon of the salt until tender.

Purée the green chiles and then the red peppers separately in a food processor until smooth. Mix the purées together. Add the potatoes and stock and process in 2-cup batches for another minute, or until smooth. Add the remaining salt, the black pepper, and garlic and process again. Press the purée through a fine sieve. Discard the contents of the sieve.

Heat the purée in a saucepan. Serve hot, garnish each bowl with sour cream, the tumbleweed greens, and one lime wedge.
Serves 6

NOTE: If using New Mexico green chiles you may want to use the mild variety. New Mexico chiles tend to be hotter than Anaheim chiles and will make this soup quite hot. If you want soup that is less spicy, use 8 green chiles with 6 red bell peppers.

INDIAN FRYBREAD

This bread is served during some of the Pueblo Feast Days, but more commonly at gatherings of Diné (Navajo) families and at their ceremonies. Many Diné eat frybread with almost every meal. It is found at all public Indian events, including dances and powwows. You can usually buy frybread at these events, served plain with powdered sugar sprinkled on it or made into an Indian Taco (page 143). Both ways, it's delicious.

4 cups flour
2 tablespoons baking powder
1 teaspoon salt
2 cups warm water
Vegetable oil or shortening, melted, for frying

Mix the flour, baking powder, and salt in a large bowl. Gradually stir in the water until the dough becomes soft and pliable without sticking to the bowl.

Knead the dough on a lightly floured surface or in the bowl for 5 minutes, folding the outer edges of the dough toward the center.

Return the dough to the bowl, cover with a clean towel, and let rest for 30 minutes to allow it to rise.

Shape the dough into egg-sized balls and roll out to a thickness of ½ inch (or thinner, for crispier bread) on a lightly floured board. It is traditional to use your hands, but a rolling pin can be used as well. Try it with your hands and then, if you are having difficulty, roll the dough out.

Place a piece of dough between your hands and pat if from hand to hand as you would a tortilla or pizza dough, until it has stretched to 8 to 12 inches in diameter. Repeat with the rest of the dough.

With your finger, poke a small hole in the center of each piece, to prevent bursting during frying.

Pour about 1½ inches of oil into a large frying pan or saucepan (the saucepan's greater depth will prevent the oil from splattering) and heat over medium heat until the oil is hot but not smoking.

Carefully place a piece of the dough in the hot oil, slipping it in gently to avoid splattering. Cook until the dough turns golden brown and puffs. Turn over with 2 forks and cook until both sides are golden brown.

Remove and drain on paper towels until the excess oil is absorbed. Repeat this process with each piece of dough. Keep warm between two clean kitchen towels in the oven set on low. Serve immediately.
Makes about 16 frybreads

ADOBE BREAD

This is an adaptation of the traditional recipe that is still being used by many Native American families. Traditionally, it is baked in an outdoor adobe oven. Among the Pueblos, women still make many loaves at a time, especially for Feast Day ceremonies. Here, it is baked in a conventional oven. In Santa Fe, you can buy loaves of this freshly baked bread on the plaza from Native American vendors, otherwise you can make it yourself.

1 package (¼ ounce) active dry yeast
¼ cup lukewarm water
1 teaspoon salt
3 tablespoons lard or vegetable shortening, melted
1 cup cold water
4½ cups flour

In a large bowl, soften the yeast in the lukewarm water. Mix the salt, 2 tablespoons of the lard, and the cold water together and add it to the yeast mixture.

Sift in the flour gradually, beating well after each addition for a smooth consistency. You will probably have to knead in the final cup of flour.

Shape the dough into a ball, crush lightly with the remaining lard, and cover with a dry cloth. Set the bowl in a warm, dry place until it has doubled in bulk, about 1 hour.

Punch the dough down and, on a floured board, knead it for 5 minutes. Shape into 2 round loaves and place on a well-greased baking sheet. Cover with a dry cloth and set aside to rise another 45 minutes.

Preheat the oven to 400°. Bake the loaves on the baking sheet for 50 minutes, until they are light brown and sound hollow when tapped.
Makes 2 round loaves

NOTE: To make bread crumbs, simply rub the crust and/ or inside of fresh Adobe Bread between your fingers to a fine crumb, or place day-old bread in a food processor and grind into crumbs. One loaf makes 2 to 3 cups of bread crumbs.

Opposite: Ann Taliman (Santa Clara Pueblo) baking adobe oven bread (top). Horno adobe brick ovens at Taos Pueblo (bottom).

BATTER-DIPPED CHILES WITH FIERY BEAN SAUCE

Unlike the chile relleno that is stuffed, breaded, and then fried, this version is simply a roasted chile that is dipped in a light batter and then fried. Served with the bean sauce, these chiles make a wonderful spicy dish that's great for vegetarians, or a great side dish for lunch or dinner.

1 cup dried pinto beans, or 2½ cups canned beans, drained
12 green New Mexico or Anaheim chiles (see note, page 67)
½ cup water
1 egg, beaten
1 cup flour
½ cup heavy cream
¾ cup chicken stock (page 198)
6 whole red chiles de árbol
1 teaspoon finely chopped chile pequín
2 cups vegetable oil

To prepare the dried beans, soak overnight in water to cover. The following day, rinse the beans with cold water and place in a saucepan with enough fresh water to cover. Bring to a boil over high heat, then decrease the heat and simmer for several hours, until the skins split. Add water when necessary to keep the beans from drying, and stir occasionally to prevent burning and sticking. Remove from the heat and drain.

Roast the green chiles (page 61), then peel, seed, and devein them. Leave the chiles whole with their stems on.

While the beans are cooking, prepare the batter. In a bowl, mix together the water, egg, flour, and heavy cream, then set aside for 1 hour.

In a saucepan over moderate heat, combine the beans, stock, chiles de árbol, and chile pequín. Decrease the heat to low and simmer, covered, 10 minutes, stirring occasionally to prevent burning.

Heat the oil in a wok or deep skillet over high heat until very hot but not smoking.

Dip each green chile into the batter, making sure it is completely covered. Gently drop the chiles into the hot oil and fry each side for 1 to 2 minutes, until light golden brown. Drain on paper towels and serve immediately with the fiery bean sauce.

Serves 6

Fresh Chile and Corn Fritters with Julienne of Tart Indian Apples

Although many Native American cooks dry foods for use through-out the year, especially the winter months, the fresh taste of recently harvested food is always preferred: the corn is sweeter, the chiles spicier, and the apples are tart. During the late summer, when these fruits and vegetables are harvested, a dish such as this, which combines an array of different flavors, is a favorite.

Chile and Corn Fritters
4 green New Mexico or Anaheim chiles
3 cups fresh corn kernels, scraped from the cob
3 green serrano chiles, seeded and chopped
1 teaspoon salt
½ teaspoon white pepper
3 tablespoons flour
¾ cup vegetable oil

Julienne of Apples
1 tablespoon unsalted butter
6 small green apples, cored and julienned (do not peel)
½ teaspoon celery seed

To make the fritters, roast the chiles (page 61), then peel, seed, and dice them.

Process the corn in a food processor until it resembles a purée, about 2 minutes. Scrape down with a spatula and process for another minute.

In a bowl, mix together the corn purée, the chopped green chiles, serranos, salt, and pepper. Slowly add the flour, small amounts at a time, while stirring.

In a saucepan, heat the oil over high heat. Using a large cook's spoon or serving spoon, gently drop spoonfuls of the batter into the hot oil. When the edges are brown after about 2 minutes, turn the fritters over and cook for another 2 minutes. Remove the fritters and allow them to drain on paper towels.

To make the julienne, in another saucepan over medium-high heat, melt the butter, add the apples and celery seed, and sauté for about 3 minutes, until they begin to soften. Serve hot with the fritters.
Makes 12 to 15 fritters; serves 4 to 5 as an appetizer

CHILE TURNOVERS

In northern Arizona, this recipe is called a turnover. In south-ern Arizona and New Mexico, where the Spanish influence is strong, these turnovers are called empanadas, which literally means "to fill." The ingredients vary somewhat, depending on which part of the Southwest they are made in. This recipe resembles the traditional northern Arizona turnover, made with beef and green chiles. These are delicious as a snack, for lunch, or for dinner. They taste best hot from the oven.

FILLING

3 green New Mexico or Anaheim chiles
1 tablespoon unsalted butter
1 pound lean ground beef
1 medium onion, finely chopped
1 cup peeled and finely chopped carrot
2 cloves garlic, finely chopped
1 teaspoon salt
2 tablespoons red chile powder
¼ cup finely chopped fresh tarragon

DOUGH

4 cups flour
½ teaspoon salt
3 tablespoons baking powder
½ cup vegetable shortening
1½ cups milk
2 eggs, beaten, for egg wash

Sprigs of fresh herbs, for garnish (optional)

To make the filling, roast the green chiles using the open flame method (page 61), then peel, seed, devein, and chop them. Melt the butter in a skillet over medium heat, then add the ground beef. Brown the meat for 7 to 10 minutes. Pour off any excess fat. Add the onion, green chiles, carrot, garlic, salt, red chile powder, and tarragon. Sauté for another 5 minutes over medium heat, until the onions are translucent and the flavor of the chiles has penetrated into the meat. Remove from the heat and set aside to cool while making the dough.

To prepare the dough, in a bowl, sift together the flour, salt, and baking powder. Add the shortening and work it into the dry ingredients with your hands or a large spoon. Add the milk and mix together until the dough is soft and pliable, being careful not to over-work it.

Preheat the oven to 400°. On a floured work sur-face, roll out the dough into circles 6 inches in diameter, no thicker than ⅛ inch. Fill each circle with 2 to 3 table-spoons of filling, brush a little of the beaten eggs around the edges of the circle, and fold the dough over, sealing the edges together with a fork. You will now have a half circle of dough filled with the meat and chile filling.

Lay the turnovers on a lightly greased cookie sheet and brush the top of each with the remaining egg wash. Bake for 20 to 25 minutes, until golden brown.

Remove from the oven. Brush more egg wash on the top of each turnover and place an herb leaf or sprig on top. Return to the oven and bake for an additional 5 minutes. If you do not wish to add herbs, omit this step and cook for 5 minutes longer.

Remove from the oven and serve hot.

Serves 6 to 8

INDIAN SALSA

Almost every Pueblo and tribe in the Southwest has a recipe for some kind of Indian salsa, which is used as a condiment with almost every meal. All of the salsas I've tasted on my travels were spicy to my palate; this recipe is a combination of the many I tried. If you find it too hot for your taste, cut the number of jalapeños in half. I serve this salsa with the Cornsicles (page 45) as an appetizer.

11 tomatillos, husked, rinsed, and finely chopped
4 large ripe tomatoes, finely chopped
¾ cup chopped onion
3 cloves garlic, finely chopped
6 jalapeño peppers, seeded, deveined, and finely
    chopped
½ cup finely chopped fresh cilantro
2 teaspoons freshly squeezed lime juice
1 teaspoon salt

Toss together all of the ingredients in a bowl. Allow to marinate for 1 hour to bring out the full flavor. Serve cold or at room temperature as a condiment with any of your favorite recipes.
Makes about 3½ cups

CHILE PEPPER JELLY

Chile Pepper Jelly is a fantastic way to preserve chiles. It makes a delicious condiment at any meal.

1 tablespoon chopped serrano chiles
1 cup diced New Mexico or Anaheim chiles
1 medium green bell pepper, seeded, deveined, and diced
1¼ cups red wine vinegar
5 cups sugar
6 ounces liquid pectin, or 1 package (1¾ ounces) powdered pectin

Combine the chiles and bell pepper with the vinegar in a food processor. Process 3 minutes, until puréed.

Put the purée and sugar in a saucepan. Bring the mixture to a hard rolling boil over medium-high heat, stirring constantly. Remove from the heat, skim the foam from the top, and discard, and add the pectin. Return to the heat and bring to a hard boil for 2 minutes (see note), stirring constantly. Remove from the heat and stir constantly for 5 minutes.

As it cools, the jelly will begin to thicken. Pour it into clean, sterilized 8-ounce jars, leaving a ¼-inch space at the top. Seal as desired.
Makes six 8-ounce jars of jelly

NOTE: When cooking this recipe at high altitudes, you will need to add 1 minute of cooking time per 1,000 feet of altitude to the time listed above.

FRESH TOMATO SAUCE

Unlike many tomato sauces, this one is rich and thick and works well as a base for many recipes in addition to pizzas.

24 fresh tomatoes, peeled, seeded, and quartered
1 small onion, diced
3 cloves garlic, finely chopped
2 tablespoons olive oil
½ teaspoon salt
½ teaspoon white pepper
1 bay leaf
1 tablespoon finely chopped fresh basil leaves
2 teaspoons finely chopped fresh oregano leaves

Purée the tomatoes in a food processor until smooth, approximately 1 minute.

In a large saucepan over medium heat, sauté the onion and garlic in the olive oil until the onions are translucent. Add the tomato purée, salt, pepper, bay leaf, basil, and oregano and mix together. Decrease the heat and simmer for about ½ hour, until the sauce is reduced by half and becomes a thicker paste.
Makes about 2 cups

RIO GRANDE PIZZAS

This pizza recipe was inspired by the abundance of produce that is available in northern New Mexico during the summer months. Red, ripe tomatoes are sweet and delicate in flavor; chiles range in taste from mild to hot; and fresh herbs are pungent and aromatic. These ingredients make for delicious homemade individual pizzas. Check in your own area for a local farmers' market so that you can purchase ingredients at their freshest.

4 green New Mexico or Anaheim chiles
1½ cups Fresh Tomato Sauce
6 Blue Cornmeal Tortillas (page 33), baked
5 ounces (about ½ cup) soft white goat cheese
1 bunch chives, chopped
6 thin slices Garlic Meat Jerky (see variation, page 197)
2 tablespoons chopped fresh basil leaves

Roast the chiles by the oven or open flame method (page 61), then peel, seed, devein, and chop them. (You can also use green chiles that have already been roasted and chopped, found in most grocers' freezer section.)

Preheat the oven to 400°.

Heat the tomato sauce in a saucepan over medium heat. Spoon about ¼ cup sauce over each tortilla and crumble the goat cheese, chives, and meat jerky on top.

Place the pizzas on a baking sheet and cook in the oven for 7 to 10 minutes, until the cheese is melted and the pizzas are hot. Sprinkle fresh basil on top and serve immediately.
Serves 6

VARIATION: This pizza recipe can be varied according to what you find in your garden, the farmers' market, and your imagination. Grilled rabbit, beans, tomatillos, and raw onion are all successful additions. I usually see what I can find, creating a new variation each time I make this pizza recipe.

Lamb-stuffed Green Chiles with Fresh Tomato Puree

This recipe, an adaptation of stuffed green bell peppers, combines many regional ingredients. It is a favorite of my cooking classes here in Santa Fe, as well as of many guests for whom I have prepared this dish. For a spicier flavor, cook the stuffed chiles for a bit longer in the oven.

Lamb-stuffed Green Chiles

12 firm green New Mexico mild or Anaheim chiles
1 tablespoon olive oil
⅔ cup finely chopped wild onions (see note, page 87)
  or yellow onions
1½ pounds ground lamb
1 cup Adobe Bread Crumbs (see note, page 68)
2 ripe tomatoes, diced
2 cloves garlic, minced
1 teaspoon salt
½ teaspoon white pepper
½ teaspoon dried thyme
2 bay leaves
1 tablespoon chopped fresh tarragon, or
  1 teaspoon dried

Fresh Tomato Purée

1 tablespoon olive oil
6 cloves garlic, minced
1¼ pounds tomatoes, coarsely chopped

Sour cream, for garnish (optional)

To make the stuffed chiles, roast, peel, and seed the chiles, keeping them whole for stuffing, according to the directions on page 61. Set aside.

Heat the oil in a large skillet over medium heat and sauté the onions for about 4 minutes, until translucent. Add the ground lamb and brown for 15 minutes, stirring occasionally to prevent burning. Drain off the excess fat and add the bread crumbs, tomatoes, garlic, salt, pepper, and herbs. Decrease the heat and simmer for another 15 minutes. Remove from the heat and let cool.

Slice the chiles lengthwise, spread them open on a work surface, and generously stuff each chile with the lamb mixture. Place the stuffed chiles with the open-side down on an oiled baking pan and set aside.

To make the purée, heat the oil in a saucepan over medium-low heat. Add the garlic and sauté for 1 minute. Add the tomatoes and cook for another 15 minutes, stirring occasionally to prevent burning, until the excess liquid evaporates. The sauce will reduce and thicken. At this point, you can pour the sauce through a fine sieve to remove the skins or you can serve the sauce as it is (most of the students in my cooking classes prefer this sauce in its more rustic state). Set aside.

Preheat the oven to 350°. Place the stuffed chiles on the baking pan in the oven and heat until hot, 5 to 10 minutes. Serve immediately with the tomato purée. Garnish with sour cream, if desired.
Serves 6

GROWN FROM THE VINE

TOMATOES, SQUASH, PUMPKINS, AND MELONS

NATIVE AMERICANS of the Southwest have a particular talent for the propagation of vine-grown fruits and vegetables. Most vine-grown fruits and squash are harvested in the late summer and throughout the fall. When harvest season arrives in the Southwest, there is an abundance of squash, melons, and tomatoes. They are roasted and dried, or simply dried in the desert sun, and stored away for later use. With the advent of freezers, much produce can be roasted and then frozen for months, if not the whole winter season.

Squash (*Cucurbita* spp.) was one of the most important New World crops, along with corn (*Zea mays*) and beans (*Phaseolus* spp.), which are believed to have been domesticated in Mesoamerica sometime between 7000 and 3000 B.C.[i] Much of the relevant data are from the semiarid Tehuacán Valley in central Mexico and from dry caves in interior Tamaulipas, eastern Mexico.[ii] Other crops include avocados, green-striped cushaw squash (*Cucurbita mixta*), and possibly cotton (*Gossypium* spp.).

Scientists believe that during this time most people probably lived in small groups and subsisted primarily on hunting and gathering, supplementing their diets with these crops.[iii]

As sedentary life became more widely practiced new crops were added to the diet, including bottle gourds (*Lagenaria siceraria*), warty squash (*Cucurbita moschata*), and the common bean (*Phaseolus vulgaris*). As more time passed, domesticates such as the jack bean (*Canavalia ensiformis*), tepary beans (*Phaseolus acutifolius*), and pumpkin and summer squashes (both *Cucurbita pepo*) were introduced. The earliest known squash in the Southwest—*Cucurbita pepo*—was a versatile plant that provided edible seeds and fruit with thick rinds that were used as tools and containers. The squash from Southwestern sites that date before about 900 A.D. are all of a single variety. After that, several varieties of *Cucurbita pepo* were grown, but it is not known whether these reflect local development or were the result of further contact with Mexico.[iv]

Like many edible New World plants, squash is eaten in different stages of development, from the yellow flowers and the shoot-tips to the immature fruit, the ripe fruit (fresh or dried into strips), and finally the ripe seeds. Squash were valued for their hard shells, used for containers (their domestication probably took place before the knowledge of pottery), and for their protein- and oil-rich seeds.[v] Original distribution of squash in the wild can be traced to the range of various species of bees of the genus *Peponapis,* whose sole source of nectar and pollen was the squash. As unlikely as it may seem, insect distributions have contributed to culinary history. Acorn squash, zucchini, summer squash, the yellow-flowered decorative gourds, and some pumpkins are all of the species *Cucurbita pepo.* The other exclusively northern hemisphere squash is *Cucurbita mixta,* the cushaw found from the southwestern United States all the way down to Costa Rica.[vi] One of the oldest and most popular squash amongst the Hopi is the green-striped cushaw, which is grown each year from seeds of earlier crops.[vii]

Squash has been an important part of the Native American diet for thousands of years. Squash blossoms are considered a delicacy, especially among the Zuni. If picked early in the morning before the flowers open up to the sun, squash blossoms can be fried, blanched, or stuffed, adding a special dimension to many dishes. Male blossoms are primarily the ones harvested. Their sole purpose is to pollinate the female blossoms, and as long as several are left in the squash patch, the female blossoms can be pollinated by the bees and produce squash throughout the summer season. Squash blossoms are a favorite of mine, and I cook with them every summer both at home and in my cooking classes. The farmers' market in Santa Fe sells them during July, August, and part of September, depending on the weather. Check with your local farmers and ask if they will sell them to you. In some areas, squash blossoms are also called *flores de calabasas.* If you can only find the female blossoms with the baby squash attached to them, as available in some of the specialty markets, these can also be used.

Tomatoes were being eaten by the Aztecs at the time of conquest. The word *tomatl* in Nahuatl means something round and plump and was used to refer to many fruits. In Nahuatl, root words such as *tomatl* were modified by adding prefixes and suffixes, so it is difficult to determine which round and plump fruits they were referring to when the Spanish shortened the name to *tomatl.*[viii] Although technically not a vine, tomatoes are referred to as grown from the vine because of the way they produce rather long stems, which look like vines.

Tomatoes, fresh and plump, taste especially sweet in the summer. The conditions in which they are grown will determine their sweetness. They prefer rich, moist soil and warm conditions. They are most famously used in the Southwest for salsas; varying degrees of hotness come from the addition of chiles.

Melons and cantaloupes, varieties of *Cucumis melo* are Old World edibles introduced to the New World by the Spanish. Watermelons *(Citrullus vulgaris)* were sometimes referred to "horse pumpkins" by the Hopi because they smelled like a sweating horse.[ix] Tribes throughout the desert quickly adapted this melon, as did many of the Pueblos. Documentation shows that although not an aboriginal crop, these melons are mentioned in ritual songs at Santa Clara as one of the principal crops. Today, almost all of the tribes seem to grow at least two different types of watermelons: one with pinkish seeds and yellow flesh and the other with black seeds and pink flesh. The seeds of the watermelon are ground and used by the Hopi for greasing their *piki* stones on which they make a paper-thin corn bread.

Melons have always been a cool refresher in hot weather. They are served at feasts and celebrations of all kinds during the summer; they are also dried, usually in long spiral strips, and stored for later use. Dried melon is eaten as a snack throughout the winter (as is pumpkin) and it is also stewed with honey or sugar and used in desserts.

All of these wonderful vine-grown fruits and vegetables are now a part of the Southwest and its rich and pungent foods. Some of the recipes that follow are left in their traditional form, and some are contemporary versions designed for the modern kitchen. The recipes are all good and are to be enjoyed with these special ingredients that are grown from the vine.

SQUASH BLOSSOM SOUP

This light, clear soup has a subtle flowery taste that is quite unusual. Serve it in the summer when squash blossoms are readily available. Plan to use squash blossoms the day you pick or purchase them, as they tend to wilt easily and lose their delicate form and flavor.

60 male squash blossoms (or female blossoms
    if male blossoms are not available), washed
1 tablespoon unsalted butter
½ cup chopped wild onion (see note) or
    yellow onion
2 cloves garlic, finely chopped
1 teaspoon salt
½ teaspoon white pepper
6 cups chicken stock (page 198)
18 sprigs chervil, for garnish

If using male squash blossoms, remove the stamens. Set aside. Melt the butter in a saucepan over medium heat. Add the onions and garlic and sauté until the onions are translucent. Decrease the heat to low, add the salt, pepper, and squash blossoms, and sauté for 3 minutes, stirring occasionally to prevent burning. Add the stock, bring to a boil over high heat, decrease the heat to low, and simmer for 10 minutes. Remove from the heat and serve hot, garnished with sprigs of chervil.
Serves 6

NOTE: The wild onion *(Allium cernuum)* grows throughout the Southwest during the spring and summer. It thrives best in moist soil and can be found at elevations of 1,000 to 10,000 feet. It grows from a basal bulb, the part of the wild onion that can be used like a regular onion in cooking and sautéing. The leaf of the wild onion is long and tubular, resembling a scallion or chive; it can be chopped and used similarly. The wild onion has edible flowers, ranging in color from white to pale pink, that make an attractive garnish.

Above: Tiffany Georgeina Morgan and Cassandra Lyn Begay (Diné) from Pinon, Arizona, harvesting squash from Tiffany's grandmother, Rita Yazzie's garden.

FRIED SQUASH BLOSSOMS
WITH CELERY SAUCE

Squash blossoms are eaten in many of the Pueblos along the Rio Grande. To the Zuni in western New Mexico, they are a great delicacy. The flowers are carefully gathered in the early morning before the blossoms open up to the sun. Male blossoms are gathered because they do not bear fruit, are larger than the female blossoms, and are better able to hold their form when used in cooking and are perfect for stuffing. Several commercial growers are willing to ship male blossoms to the consumer. Specialty markets also carry squash blossoms, and many farmers' markets sell squash blossoms when they are in season.

FRIED SQUASH BLOSSOMS

½ cup water

1 egg, beaten

1 cup flour

½ cup heavy cream

1 green New Mexico or Anaheim chile

1 tablespoon unsalted butter

1 onion, finely chopped

2 cloves garlic, finely chopped

2 tomatoes, peeled, seeded, and chopped

½ teaspoon salt

¼ teaspoon white pepper

4 ounces (about ⅓ cup) soft white goat cheese

30 squash blossoms, preferably male

2 to 3 cups vegetable oil, for frying

CELERY SAUCE

1 pound celery, leaves and stalks

3 tablespoons unsalted butter

½ teaspoon salt

To make the batter, mix together in a bowl the water, egg, flour, and cream. Set aside and let stand for 1 hour. The blossoms will fry better if the batter has time to set.

To make the sauce, cut the celery into 1-inch chunks and place in a pot with enough salted water to cover. Bring to a boil over high heat and cook for about 20 minutes, until the celery is tender.

Drain the water; place the celery in a food processor and purée. Strain through a fine sieve into a saucepan. Discard the contents of the sieve. Heat the celery purée over medium-low heat for 8 to 10 minutes, or until it has reduced by half. Add the butter and salt and stir until the sauce is smooth and shiny. Set aside and reheat to serve with the fried squash blossoms.

Using the open flame method (page 61), roast, peel, seed, and dice the green chile.

In a saucepan over medium-low heat, melt the butter and sauté the onion until it is translucent. Add the garlic and sauté for 1 more minute. Add the tomatoes, chile, salt, and pepper; stir and decrease the heat to low. Simmer for about 5 minutes, until the vegetables are soft. Stir occasionally to prevent burning. Remove from the heat and set aside. In a separate bowl, mix together the goat cheese and the sautéed vegetables. (The vegetables will still be warm and this will help soften the goat cheese.) Place the mixture in a pastry bag for filling the squash blossoms.

If using male squash blossoms, remove the stamens and discard (the stamens are edible but bitter). Fill each blossom with 1 to 2 teaspoons of the cheese and vegetable mixture, pull together the tip of the blossom, and twist it to seal in the filling. Hold the blossom by the stem and gently dip it into the batter, covering the entire blossom.

Heat the oil in a large saucepan or fryer until it is very hot but not smoking. If the oil is not hot enough the blossoms will be very oily by the time they are finished cooking. Gently drop each blossom into the oil. Fry for 1 to 2 minutes on each side, turning them once, until they are golden brown. Remove the blossoms with a slotted spoon or tongs and drain on paper towels.

Using a sharp knife, slice each blossom diagonally. If the blossoms are smaller, I usually just serve them whole. Spoon about ⅓ cup sauce onto each of the 6 plates, top with the fried squash blossoms, and serve hot.

Serves 6 as an appetizer

MESA SQUASH FRY WITH SUNFLOWER SEEDS

Sometimes called calabacitas, *this colorful squash fry is a delicious dish. There are several different variations, this one is my favorite.*

1 green New Mexico or Anaheim chile
2 tablespoons sunflower oil
2 cloves garlic, finely chopped
½ teaspoon salt
½ teaspoon black pepper
8 ears sweet yellow corn, kernels cut from the cob
4 small zucchini, cut into 2-inch-long julienne
4 yellow squash, cut into 2-inch-long julienne
1 red bell pepper, seeded, deveined, and diced
¼ cup shelled sunflower seeds

Roast the chile (page 61), then peel, seed, and coarsely chop it.

In a sauté pan, heat the oil over medium-high heat. When the oil is hot but not smoking, add the garlic, chile, salt, and black pepper. Cook for 1 to 2 minutes, stirring constantly, to allow the flavors to blend.

Add the corn, zucchini, squash, and red bell pepper. Decrease the heat and allow the vegetables to simmer for about 10 minutes, until they are tender.

Above: Two young Native girls at the Pow Wow during Indian Market.

Add the sunflower seeds and simmer for another 5 minutes. Serve hot.
Serves 6 to 8

COOKED PUMPKIN

Pumpkin is a winter squash that has been cultivated in the Southwest for hundreds of years. It ranges in size from several inches to several feet and can be round or oblong in shape. The average cooking pumpkin is usually between 10 and 25 pounds. The meat, the seeds, and the pumpkin's blossoms all are edible and can be prepared in many different ways. Pumpkin pulp is also sold in 16-ounce cans, which makes a convenient substitute for fresh cooked pumpkin in recipes. Fresh pumpkin, however, always tastes better, making it worth the effort. I usually cook several pumpkins at a time when they are in season, purée the meat, and then freeze it in plastic bags for later use so I can enjoy its delicious taste throughout the remainder of the year.

Here is the method I use to cook fresh pumpkins. Cut the pumpkin into halves or quarters, depending on the size of the pumpkin. Remove the seeds and fibers. Place the halves or quarters on a baking sheet with the cut-side down. This seals in the moisture from the pumpkin and allows it to steam while it is baking, making for moister pumpkin meat. The seeds can be also be roasted in the oven and make a delicious and healthy snack.

Preheat the oven to 350° and bake the pumpkin for 45 minutes, until it is tender. The pumpkin meat should be soft when you touch it with a fork.

Remove the pumpkin from the oven and allow it to cool. When the pumpkin has cooled, scrape the flesh from the skin. Discard the skins. Place the meat in a food processor and purée. Run through a sieve to remove any remaining fibers and use the pumpkin according to recipe instructions. If you have done a good job scraping the meat from the skins and there are no fibers, you can omit this step.

Cooked pumpkin will keep about 1 week in a nonmetal, covered container in the refrigerator and several months in the freezer.

Two pounds of fresh pumpkin—skin, seeds, and fiber removed—makes about 2 cups of cooked pumpkin.

PUMPKIN MARMALADE WITH
HOMEMADE POTATO CHIPS

Here, harvested pumpkin is made into a marmalade that can be sealed in jars and enjoyed throughout the entire year. It is served with homemade potato chips, but it also tastes delicious with yuca root (Manihot utilissima) made into chips. Yuca root is a starchy staple from the tropics that tapioca is also based on. I find yuca root, sometimes called cassava root, in my local supermarket here in Santa Fe.

PUMPKIN MARMALADE

1½ cups water
3 cups cooked pumpkin (opposite page)
6 ounces liquid pectin
5 cups sugar

HOMEMADE POTATO CHIPS

3 cups vegetable oil
3 large russet potatoes or yuca root, peeled and sliced
   ⅛ inch thick

To make the marmalade, combine the water, pumpkin, and pectin in a saucepan and stir. Bring to a hard rolling boil over medium-high heat while stirring constantly to prevent scorching. Add the sugar, continue stirring, and return to a hard rolling boil for 8 minutes (see note) or until it reaches about 200° on a candy thermometer. Remove from the heat, skim any foam from the top, and pour into hot, sterilized jars. Seal as desired. Allow to set and cool.

To make the potato chips, heat the oil in a skillet over medium-high heat until it is almost smoking. Add enough potato slices to cover the bottom of the pan and fry for 1 to 2 minutes on each side until golden brown and crisp. Thinner slices will fry more quickly than thicker pieces. Repeat the process until all of the slices are fried.

Blot the chips on paper towels to remove the excess oil. Serve with the pumpkin marmalade.
Makes about six 8-ounce jars of marmalade

NOTE: If you are preparing this recipe at higher altitudes, you will need to add 1 minute of cooking time per 1,000 feet of altitude.

PUMPKIN CORN SOUP WITH GINGER-LIME CREAM

This recipe is easy to prepare and utilizes two very basic ingredients in Southwestern cooking: pumpkin and corn. It is a delicious and rich soup, and the Ginger-lime Cream adds a refreshing zest.

PUMPKIN CORN SOUP

3 cups corn kernels (fresh if in season,
    otherwise frozen)
2 cloves garlic, finely chopped
¾ teaspoon salt
¼ teaspoon white pepper
3 cups chicken stock (page 198)
3 cups cooked pumpkin (page 92)

GINGER-LIME CREAM

Juice and zest of 2 limes
1 tablespoon peeled and grated fresh ginger
½ cup heavy cream

To make the soup, in a covered pot, cook the corn kernels with a little water until soft, about 10 minutes. In a food processor, process the corn until smooth, about 2 minutes. Pass through a sieve and discard the skins.

Combine the corn purée, garlic, salt, pepper, and stock in a saucepan and bring to a boil over medium-high heat. Decrease the heat to low, add the pumpkin, and cook for 10 minutes while stirring.

To make the cream, in another saucepan, cook the lime juice and ginger for 2 minutes over medium heat. Remove from the heat and pour through a sieve to remove the ginger.

In a bowl, combine the ginger and lime juice mixture, the lime zest (save some for garnish), and cream. Whip until the mixture has soft peaks.

Top each bowl of soup with a dollop of cream and garnish with the remaining lime zest. Serve immediately.
Serves 6

PUMPKIN-PIÑON BREAD WITH PUMPKIN SAUCE AND ICE CREAM

This moist, dense bread can be eaten alone for a snack or for breakfast. With the addition of the Pumpkin Sauce and Ice Cream, the bread can also be enjoyed as a wonderfully rich dessert.

PUMPKIN SAUCE AND ICE CREAM

20 egg yolks

2 cups sugar

2 quarts milk

½ vanilla bean, split lengthwise

2 cups cooked pumpkin (page 92)

⅛ teaspoon ground cloves

⅛ teaspoon grated nutmeg

¼ teaspoon ground cinnamon

PUMPKIN-PIÑON BREAD

2 cups flour

1 teaspoon baking soda

½ teaspoon salt

1½ cups sugar

2 teaspoons ground cinnamon

3 eggs, beaten

¾ cup milk

½ cup sunflower oil

1 teaspoon vanilla extract

2 cups cooked pumpkin (page 92)

1 cup roasted piñons (see note)

To make the pumpkin sauce and ice cream, beat the egg yolks and sugar together in a bowl. Set aside.

Heat the milk and vanilla bean in a saucepan over high heat. Stir constantly until it almost reaches the boiling point. Remove from the heat. Remove the vanilla bean and slowly whisk the hot milk into the egg and sugar mixture. Return the mixture to the saucepan over medium-low heat and stir constantly for about 10 minutes to thicken the mixture. Do not allow the mixture to boil or it will curdle.

Once the mixture is thick enough to coat the back of a spoon, remove it from the heat and add the pumpkin. Stir until completely mixed.

Put 2 cups of the mixture in a bowl and add to it the cloves, nutmeg, and cinnamon. Mix together well and set the bowl in another bowl filled with ice, stirring occasionally until cool, then refrigerate. This sauce will last up to 5 days refrigerated in a covered container.

Pour the remainder of the egg-pumpkin mixture into another bowl. Set the bowl in another bowl of ice, stirring occasionally, until it has cooled completely, then place in an ice cream machine and freeze according to the manufacturer's instructions. The ice cream will last several weeks in a covered container in the freezer.

To make the bread, preheat the oven to 350°. Sift together the flour, baking soda, salt, sugar, and cinnamon.

In a separate bowl, combine the eggs, milk, oil, and vanilla and mix well. Stir in the pumpkin purée and the dry ingredients, mix well, and then fold in the piñons.

Pour the batter into two greased 5 by 9-inch loaf pans and bake for 45 minutes, until the bread springs back when touched.

Serve with the pumpkin sauce and ice cream as a dessert.

Makes 2 cups sauce, ½ gallon ice cream, and two 5 by 9-inch loaves of bread; serves 12 as a dessert

NOTE: To roast the piñons, also known as pine nuts, place them in a dry frying pan over medium heat and stir constantly so that they brown evenly, for 3 to 5 minutes. No butter or oil is needed because the nuts contain natural oils.

TESUQUE PUMPKIN COOKIES

Most of the Pueblos in New Mexico are relatively close to one another. Because of their proximity, many of the women bring prepared foods over to other Pueblos during Feast Days or other celebrations. As a result, each Pueblo has developed its own version of certain recipes. I learned this particular recipe from some of the women at Tesuque Pueblo just north of Santa Fe. The cookies are delicious and not too sweet and will disappear faster than you can imagine!

2 cups sugar
2 cups vegetable shortening
2 cups cooked pumpkin (page 92)
2 eggs, beaten
2 teaspoons vanilla extract
4 cups flour
2 teaspoons baking soda
1 teaspoon salt
1 teaspoon grated nutmeg
½ teaspoon ground allspice
2 cups raisins
1 cup chopped walnuts

Preheat the oven to 350°. Grease a large cookie sheet.

In a large bowl, cream together the sugar and shortening. Add the pumpkin, eggs, and vanilla and beat until smooth.

In a separate bowl, combine the flour, baking soda, salt, nutmeg, and allspice.

Slowly add the dry ingredients to the pumpkin mixture, small amounts at a time, until completely mixed together. Stir in the raisins and walnuts.

Drop tablespoons of the dough roughly 2 inches apart on the cookie sheet. Bake for 12 to 15 minutes, until golden brown.

Makes about 7 dozen cookies

SUMMER MELON FRUIT SALAD
WITH PRICKLY PEAR SYRUP

The Southwest produces an abundance of melon varieties. Many of the different Pueblos and reservations have their favorites and grow only those specific varieties. Santa Fe is fortunate because during the summer months farmers from all over northern New Mexico bring their varieties of delicious melons to sell. See what your area's farmers can grow for you. For this recipe, if you can't find yellow watermelon, use pink. This recipe is cool and refreshing and is a particular favorite of mine.

1 muskmelon or cantaloupe
10 fresh Indian peaches, or 5 commercially grown
    peaches (see note)
1 large prickly pear cactus pad (nopale)
¼ yellow watermelon
Mint leaves, for garnish
¾ cup Prickly Pear Syrup (page 121)

Cut the muskmelon in half and scoop out the seeds. Scoop the melon into 1-inch balls and place in a bowl. Cut the peaches in half, or if using larger peaches, cut into slices. Add to the melon balls. Trim the cactus pad (see page 118), cut into strips, and blanch in boiling salted water for 1 to 2 minutes. Rinse the pads under cool water to remove their gum; drain well. Toss together with the fruits.

Slice the watermelon into ½-inch slices and from each slice cut 1½-inch triangles, removing the seeds as you cut. (I have found that when you slice watermelon into pieces this size it is easier to make sure there are no seeds left.) Toss the watermelon with the other fruit.

Garnish with the mint leaves and serve with the Prickly Pear Syrup.
Serves 12 as a salad or dessert

NOTE: Indian peaches are grown in the desert by a dry-farming method and tend to be smaller than commercially grown fruits.

WATERMELON JUICE

Tribes all over the Southwest grow several different kinds of watermelons, the most popular of which are the watermelons with the pink flesh and black seeds and the ones with yellow flesh and light pink seeds. Both are sweet and juicy and make a refreshing drink for warm weather. Watermelons were, and still are, given as gifts at ceremonies, especially among the Pueblo People. Watermelon seeds, besides being replanted for the following year's crops, are also ground into a mealy paste and used to grease the piki stones that are used for making traditional piki bread.

1 10-pound watermelon, chilled

Slice the watermelon lengthwise into slices 1 to 2 inches thick. Carefully cut away the rind and discard. Place as much flesh as will fit into a food processor and process until smooth, about 15 seconds. Press through a fine sieve and discard the seeds and pulp. Pour the juice into a pitcher. Repeat this process until all the watermelon has been blended and sieved. A vegetable juicer can also be used to make watermelon juice. Follow the same steps as above. Chill and serve cold.

Makes about 10 cups; serves 6 to 8

SWEET WATERMELON ICE

This recipe makes a refreshing ice that is perfect for hot weather.

2 cups fresh Watermelon Juice (above)
3 tablespoons sugar
2 tablespoons freshly squeezed lemon juice

Pour the watermelon juice into a shallow glass baking dish. Add the sugar and lemon juice and stir well. Place the dish in the freezer and chill.

Stir the liquid every 30 minutes until it has frozen into grainy ice crystals. The process should take about 4 hours, depending on the temperature of your freezer. You can also use an ice cream maker and freeze according to the manufacturer's directions.

Serve immediately, or store in the freezer in a covered container for up to several weeks.

Makes about 3 cups; serves 6

NATIVE HARVEST

WILD GREENS, CACTI, FRUIT, AND HERBS

WILD PLANTS have played an essential, even pivotal, role in shaping the lives of Native Peoples of the Southwest. This role dates back to prehistoric times and continues today. The largest cactus in the United States, the characteristic plant of the Sonoran Desert, is the saguaro *(Cereus giganteus, Carnegiea gigantea)*. The harvest of the juicy, crimson colored fruit during the summer months was—and is—so important to the Akimiel O'odham (Pima) and the Tohono O'odham (Papago) that it signaled the beginning of the new calendar year for both tribes.[i] The desert peoples became dependent upon the fruits and seeds of this cactus, which had co-evolved with birds, bats, rodents, harvester ants, and other insects over hundreds of thousands of years.[ii] Many ceremonies have been developed around this giant cactus.

Few places in North America rival the enormous plant and animal diversity found in the Southwest. Thousands of wild plant species have been recorded. High plant and animal diversity is what might have been a major key in drawing Pueblo people eastward. Certainly this accounts for population growth in the region along the Rio Grande from the time of Pueblo settlement after about A.D. 1300. Besides providing ample sources of food, high biodiversity ensured a broad selection of plants for fiber, implements, and the construction of dwellings. This diversity also offered the wide spectrum of plants whose medicinal properties formed the basis of American Indian herbal medicine, so vital for the well-being of ancestral Puebloans and widely relied upon in the present.

Most modern anthropologists assume that the gathering of wild plant foods for sustenance and medicinal and spiritual purposes has always been a part of the lives of ancestral American Indians. Plant carbohydrates are known to have provided a valuable, if not essential, nutritional supplement in the diet of virtually every culture that has subsisted primarily on meat. Wild plants began to take on greater importance as a source for human food soon after the climate warmed and the vegetation and fauna underwent substantial changes. Noted paleoecologist Paul S. Martin suggests that the setting was ripe for early hunters to "begin their 7,000-year experiment with native plants, leading to increasingly skillful techniques of harvesting and gathering, to the domestication of certain weedy camp-followers, and within the last 1,000 years, to the widespread adoption of flood plain agriculture."[iii]

A number of adaptive mechanisms enable plants to withstand arid conditions. In order to survive the stressful dry environment, intensely hot in summer and harshly cold in winter, plants of this region have undergone rapid evolutionary specialization. Many plants of the desert have become chemical factories, producing compounds that help them to survive. Some plants, drought evaders, remain inactive during dry periods and photosynthesize only when moisture becomes available. These include desert annuals that produce seeds with the ability to remain viable for long periods of drought and perennial plants that store water and nutrients in bulbs and rhizomes. Drought-resistant desert shrubs persist through drought periods by shedding most of their leaves, stems, and rootlets, which reduces their activity and water requirements. Other desert plants have the ability to minimize water loss. And even others, such as cacti and succulents, can store water internally. *Phreatophytes,* drought-resistant plants, have specialized root systems and long taproots that enable them to use ground water.[iv]

Most traditional Native Americans believe that people, plants, animals, and spirits are all interconnected in an unbroken circle of being. Many wild plants are sacred to modern Native People as well. Native People make an offering, before harvesting wild plants. Plants

Above: Debi Breen harvesting ripened prickly pear fruit.

are not harvested randomly or wastefully. Rather, they are picked as needed, and no more are picked than are necessary. In the Diné (Navajo) way, a prayer is offered to the largest and healthiest plant, along with an explanation of why its neighbor will be harvested. Afterward, the plant remains are buried with a final prayer. Every plant is sacred, and for the plants to help us they must be respected.

The aridity of the desert can cause a scarcity of many foods, but the wild plants that nature has given to this region are hardy enough to survive the long droughts and cold winters. Each spring, the cacti bud, the fruits ripen, and the herbs and greens sprout anew. These signs of spring coincide with warmer days, increased sunshine, and a new beginning to the harvesting year.

Many greens grow wild in all parts of the Southwest, along highways and in pastures, amid desert rocks, and beside planted gardens. Wild greens, such as lamb's-quarter *(Chenopodium album),* also called wild spinach; dandelion greens *(Taraxacum officinale);* mustard *(Descurainia pinnata);* wild mint *(Mentha arvensis),* purslane *(Portulaca oleracea),* called *verdolagas* throughout New Mexico and *peehala* by the Hopi; and pigweed *(Amaranthus palmerii),* or *quelites* as it is called in Spanish, can all be harvested in the springtime. Most of these greens are harvested young, in early spring before the plant has flowered or the characteristic bitter taste becomes too strong. Tumbleweed grows all over the Southwest. Tender young shoots from the tumbleweed plant *(Salsola iberica / Salsola kali)* are harvested in the spring, when the plant is still young and green. It is a vegetable that is delicious in soups, stews, and salads. The small shoots are harvested when they are 2 to 3 inches tall, before they develop thorns.

Wild onion *(Allium cernuum)* and wild celery *(Cymopterus fendleri)* are harvested during the spring and summer. Indian tea *(Thelesperma megapotamicum),* also called cota or *hohoise* by the Hopi, is harvested in the late spring and summer months. Virtually all of the Pueblo tribes, as well as the Hopi, Diné, and Apache, know this plant and consider it the best of several wild plant species for making tea. The flowers and stems of this plant are harvested, then tied into small bundles and dried for use throughout the year.

Many fruits exist in the wild. Cultivated fruits such as peaches, apricots, plums, cherries, and apples are harvested annually. These cultivated fruits that are grown in the desert without irrigation by a dry-farming method tend to be smaller than commercially grown fruits but are very sweet and tasty. The fruits grown with irrigation in parts of northern New Mexico along the Rio Grande are larger. During July, August, and September, the fruits ripen and are enjoyed fresh or dried, or are made into jellies and syrups.

Squawberry *(Rhus trilobata),* a wild berry also called lemonade berry, is harvested in the summer months and is made into a refreshing beverage; it is also ground and used to flavor sauces. Wild currants *(Ribes inebrians),* wild gooseberry *(Ribes inerme),* and chokecherry *(Prunus virginiana)* are usually found at higher elevations. They are harvested in late summer when the berries are bright to deep red, in some cases almost black, and very smooth. Few are eaten fresh when they are in season; the majority are dried for winter use. These berries are quite common, and remains of pits have been found at several Anasazi sites in northwestern New Mexico.[v]

The southern deserts are rich in cacti, and there are many different types that produce wonderful edible fruits and blossoms. The yucca *(Yucca baccata* and *Yucca elata),* found on mesas and foothills, blooms from May through September. Its fruit, referred to as banana yucca, can be eaten fresh from the plant or cooked and eaten as a vegetable. Yucca has been used in many different ways and probably had greater economic importance to Indians of the Southwest than any other group of wild plants.[vi] Fibers from the yucca have been used for manufacturing string and rope, and the use of yucca fiber for matting and basketry was—and is—widespread. An extract made from the saponin-rich yucca roots is the equivalent of soap for virtually all Indians living in the Southwest. It is used ceremonially for washing the hair by many tribes. And the yucca fibers are still used by women to make brushes for rendering their designs on pottery.

The *cholla* cactus *(Opuntia imbricata)* produces a bright yellow and sometimes light green bud or fruit that is still gathered with tongs, before the plant produces a brilliant magenta flower, by many tribes in the Southwest. The bud or fruit is then cooked and eaten as a vegetable. A 2-tablespoon serving contains as much calcium as a glass of milk.[vii] Other important succulents are the ocotillo *(Fouquieria splendens),* the barrel cactus *(Ferocactus wislizenii),* and the agave *(Agave parryi* and *Agave palmeri),* all of which have been harvested for centuries by the Natives from the southern desert regions.

The most popular edible cactus is the prickly pear *(Opuntia phaeacantha* and *Opuntia engelmanii),* which produces a reddish-magenta fruit in late summer to early fall. The tangy pulp is used for juices, jellies, preserves, and fruit ices. The pads of this cactus, known as *nopales,* are picked when young and green and are eaten as a vegetable. Scraped clean of their spines, they can be eaten in a variety of dishes. The filleted pads are effective drawing poultices. The gel in the flesh is extremely effective on contusions, bruises, and burns. Recent studies show that the folk use of prickly pear for diabetes is clinically verifiable.

The desert is rich with native plants that have been harvested and used for food, medicine, and spiritual rituals by the Native Peoples of the Southwest for thousands of years. This native harvest is an important part of the lives of the peoples from this region today, as it has been for centuries.

Opposite: Yucca (Yucca baccata) *in bloom during spring.*

FRESH HERB JELLY

There are many wild herbs indigenous to the Southwest. Unfortunately, they may be difficult to obtain in other parts of the country, if they are available at all. This recipe has been adapted to include herbs that are available in commercial markets. You can also experiment with other fresh herbs according to your own taste. I usually make this with a combination of herbs from my garden and wild herbs that are in season.

2 cups water
¾ cup freshly squeezed lemon juice
1 (1¾-ounce) package powdered pectin
4 cups sugar
¼ cup finely chopped fresh chives
¼ cup finely chopped fresh thyme leaves
¼ cup finely chopped fresh oregano leaves
¼ cup finely chopped fresh basil leaves
¼ cup finely chopped fresh tarragon leaves

In a large saucepan, stir together the water, lemon juice, and pectin. Scrape the sides of the pan to make sure all of the pectin has dissolved.

Place the saucepan over high heat and bring to a boil. Stir constantly to prevent scorching. Add the sugar and herbs while stirring. Bring the mixture to a full rolling boil for 4 minutes (see note), then remove from the heat. Skim the foam off the top of the mixture and pour into clean, sterilized jars. Seal with paraffin, if desired, and allow to set overnight.

If the herb jelly does not set overnight, remove the paraffin and reheat the mixture over high heat. Bring to a hard rolling boil for an additional 2 minutes, repour into the jars, and reseal.

Because you are working with herbs and not fruit, sometimes the pectin doesn't react the first time and needs to be reboiled.
Makes 4 8-ounce jars of jelly

NOTE: If making this jelly above sea level, you will need to add 1 minute for every 1,000 feet above sea level.

WHITE SAGE BREAD

White sage (Artemisia tridentata), *which grows wild throughout parts of Arizona and in northern New Mexico, is an aromatic herb used in a variety of dishes. If you can't find white sage, substitute culinary sage. This bread freezes well, so I suggest making several loaves at a time.*

2½ cups flour
2 teaspoons finely chopped fresh sage leaves
1 teaspoon salt
½ teaspoon baking soda
1 (¼-ounce) package active dry yeast
¼ cup lukewarm water
1 egg
1 cup cottage cheese
2 tablespoons unsalted butter, melted
Crushed roasted piñons (see note, page 97) or
    coarse salt (optional)

Opposite: Herbs and edible plants hanging to dry for later use.

In a bowl, combine the flour, sage, salt, and baking soda.

Dissolve the yeast in the lukewarm water.

In a food processor, blend the egg and cottage cheese until smooth; add 1 tablespoon of the butter and all of the yeast water, mix again, and transfer to a large bowl. Gradually add the flour mixture, kneading vigorously after each addition, until a stiff dough is formed. Cover with a dry cloth and let rest in a warm place until doubled in bulk, about 1 hour.

Punch down the dough and knead it on a lightly floured surface for about 4 minutes. Divide the dough in half and shape each part into a ball. Place the dough balls on a greased baking sheet, cover with a dry cloth, and let rise for 15 minutes more.

Preheat the oven to 350°.

Bake the bread for about 40 minutes, until it is well risen, golden, and hollow sounding when tapped. Brush the top with the remaining butter and sprinkle with crushed roasted piñons or coarse salt, if desired.
Makes 2 round loaves

TUMBLEWEEDS

Tumbleweeds *(Salsola iberica/Salsola kali)* are a signature of the Southwest and can be found growing throughout the dry and rustic terrain. With their coarse exterior, it is almost hard to believe that these plants can be eaten. However, after the first rains in the spring, new, young tumbleweed shoots sprout up. These young shoots are delicious and must be picked when they are only 2 to 3 inches tall, before they become dry and brittle and develop thornlike prickers on them. They are a delicious vegetable and are often used in salads. To harvest them yourself, pick the sprouts from the base of the stem. Wash thoroughly until all the sand and dirt are removed. Drain and pat dry.

TUMBLEWEED, PINTO BEAN, AND WILD RICE SALAD

¾ cup dried pinto beans, or 1½ cups cooked
    pinto beans
1½ cups tumbleweed greens, curly endive, or
    fennel tops, coarsely chopped
1¼ cups cooked wild rice
¾ cup sunflower oil
3 tablespoons herb-flavored red wine vinegar
2 tablespoons chopped fresh chives
2 small cloves garlic
1 tablespoon freshly squeezed lemon juice
¼ teaspoon black pepper
½ teaspoon salt
Chive blossoms, for garnish

Soak the beans overnight in water to cover. The next day, drain, rinse with cold water, and place them in a saucepan with fresh water to cover. Bring to a boil over high heat, then decrease the heat, and simmer for several hours until the beans are soft and the skins begin to split. Add water when necessary to keep the beans from drying, and stir occasionally to prevent them from burning and sticking. Remove from the heat, drain, and allow to cool.

In a bowl, toss together the beans, greens, and rice. Cover and chill in the refrigerator for at least 30 minutes.

In a blender, combine the oil, vinegar, chives, garlic, lemon juice, pepper, and salt. Blend at high speed until the chives and garlic are finely puréed.

Pour the dressing over the salad and garnish with the chive blossoms.

Serves 6

Yucca Blossom Salad with Goat Cheese Dressing

Yucca (Yucca baccata *or* Yucca elata) *has been used in many different ways and has had a greater economic importance to Pueblo Indians than any other group of wild plants growing in their region. The banana yucca (the thick, sweet fruit of the plant) formed a staple of ancient diets from this region. Corn smut, or huitlacoche, as it is called in Spanish, are the kernels from ears of corn that have developed an edible fungus similar to a mushroom. Inside each corn kernel is a moist, thick black paste. It can be dried or canned and used throughout the year. It is widely used in regional Mexican cuisine, but in the United States, it is only used by a few tribes in the Southwest.*

Yucca Blossom Salad

1 tablespoon olive oil

18 edible mushrooms or huitlacoche kernels, cleaned and chopped

30 yucca or other edible blossoms (nasturtiums work well)

6 cups mâche or Boston lettuce, stemmed

Goat Cheese Dressing

2 ounces (about ¼ cup) soft white goat cheese

¼ cup olive oil

¼ teaspoon white pepper

½ teaspoon salt

2 tablespoons herb-flavored vinegar

1 teaspoon chopped fresh thyme

To make the salad, in a sauté pan, heat the oil over medium-low heat and sauté the mushrooms for 1 to 2 minutes, stirring constantly, until tender. Set aside.

Fill a saucepan with water and bring to a boil. Blanch the yucca blossoms for 20 to 30 seconds. Remove and immediately rinse the blossoms in ice water. Drain the flowers and remove the hearts or stamens inside the blossoms and discard. Set aside. If you are using nasturtium blossoms, omit this step.

To make the dressing, blend together all of the ingredients except the vinegar. Slowly whisk in the vinegar drop by drop to avoid separating, until all the vinegar has been incorporated.

Toss the mushrooms, mâche, and yucca blossoms together with the dressing and sprinkle the thyme on top.
Serves 6

DANDELION SALAD WITH MUSTARD GREENS VINAIGRETTE

This combination of fresh greens, spicy chiles, and tender baby sweet corn is unusual and delicious.

DANDELION SALAD

2 red serrano, New Mexico red, or Anaheim red chiles
⅓ pound sunflower sprouts
20 ears baby corn (fresh if available, otherwise canned)
12 radishes
2 pounds dandelion greens or other bitter greens,
    washed and stemmed

MUSTARD GREENS VINAIGRETTE

1 bunch mustard greens, washed and stemmed
1 cup sunflower oil
2 tablespoons herb-flavored vinegar
1 teaspoon salt
½ teaspoon black pepper

To make the salad, slice the chiles diagonally, remove the seeds and veins, and stick small bunches of sprouts through the pieces.

Remove the husks and silks from the corn. Bring a small pot of water to a boil and cook the corn for 1 to 2 minutes. Drain, rinse in cold water, and let cool. (If using canned corn, simply drain and rinse.) Wash and slice the radishes.

To make the vinaigrette, place the mustard greens in a blender and add the remaining ingredients. Blend until smooth, about 2 minutes.

Toss the vinaigrette with the salad greens and serve.
Serves 6

Above: Gallina Canyon Ranch in Abiquiu, New Mexico.

COOKING WITH PRICKLY PEAR CACTUS

Prickly pear cactus *(Opuntia phaeacantha* and *Opuntia engelmannii)* grows wild throughout the southern regions of New Mexico and Arizona, where the air is warm and dry. I have, however, also seen them growing as far north as Santa Fe, and purchased them from a Native woman this past summer at the farmers' market here. These cacti have no leaves, except at the start of new growth. They have spiny, thick stems that form the body of the plant and produce lovely yellow, orange, and red roselike flowers in the spring. These mature into the prickly pear fruits in the late summer months. The young pads are cooked and eaten as a vegetable once the spines have been removed, and the ripened fruits are eaten fresh, strained as a juice, and made into syrups and jellies.

PRICKLY PEAR FRUITS

Traditionally, prickly pear fruits are harvested in the late summer. A brush made from wild grass is used to remove their fine, hairlike prickers and soft spines. To remove the prickers in a more modern way, hold the fruit with metal tongs under cold running water and scrub the prickers off with a vegetable scrubbing brush.

When selecting fruits from the marketplace, be careful to choose those that are soft but not overripe. They may range in color from greenish-yellow to bright magenta or red, the latter being the ripest and best to eat. If the spines have not been removed, be very careful when handling the fruits; the spines are small and difficult to remove from your hands. If only green fruits are available, store them at room temperature until they ripen to magenta or red.

To extract the juice from the fruits, wash them thoroughly under cold running water, cut off the ends, and cut them in half lengthwise. Place them in a food processor and purée to a fine pulp. Press the pulp through a fine sieve, using a wooden spoon or spatula to remove the seeds, which should then be discarded. Use the juice according to recipe instructions. Twelve prickly pear fruits make about 1 cup of juice. Prickly pear syrup is also available today at many specialty cooking stores.

NOTE: The prickly pear fruit, because of its deep, rich color, is traditionally used by the Diné (Navajo) as a dye for thread and yarn used in their weavings. The juice from the fruit has a very powerful color and can stain clothing, utensils, and surfaces. You may want to wear an apron while preparing prickly pear fruits and use utensils that are metal or that you don't mind getting stained.

NOPALES

Prickly pear pads, also called *nopales,* have been eaten by the Native Americans for centuries. The pads are picked from the cactus, usually in the spring, but must be handled with care; the hairlike spines that project from the pads can easily get caught in your skin.

Cactus pads are found in most Mexican markets and are becoming more and more available in supermarkets. The supermarkets here in Santa Fe carry them most of the year. It is better to choose the smaller and thicker deep-green pads because they are the most tender. Usually fresh cactus pads are sold whole. For convenience, however, they may also be purchased in jars already diced and even precooked in their natural juices.

To clean the whole pads, hold them with a kitchen towel and remove the spines using a knife and scraping the pad away from you. The rounded outside edge of the pads also needs to be removed with a small paring knife or a vegetable peeler and should then be discarded.These pads make a wonderful vegetable, are extremely healthy, and can be used in a multitude of recipes.

PRICKLY PEAR SYRUP

Prickly pears (Opuntia phaeacantha *and* Opuntia engelmannii) *also called* tunas, *are the ripened fruit from the nopal cactus. They grow in desert regions but are most abundant in the lower and warmer deserts of New Mexico and Arizona. They have a sweet, tangy flavor that makes a delicious syrup, excellent with the Blue Cornmeal and Piñon Hotcakes (page 39). It is also a wonderful topping for the Feast Days Piñon Torte (page 157) and the Picuris Indian Bread Pudding (page 126). Today, prickly pear syrup is also available commercially; see the Source Guide (page 201).*

12 prickly pear fruits
¼ cup honey
1 teaspoon freshly squeezed lemon juice

Wash and cut each prickly pear into quarters, leaving the skins on.

Place the fruit in a food processor and process until pulpy and thoroughly blended. Press the liquid through a fine sieve; discard the skin and the seeds.

Put the prickly pear juice into a saucepan with the honey and lemon juice and bring to a boil over medium-high heat. Decrease the heat and let simmer for 10 minutes, until the mixture has thickened. Remove from the heat and let cool. The syrup will thicken further as it cools. The syrup may be stored in the refrigerator for 1 to 2 weeks.

Makes about 1 cup

PRICKLY PEAR ICE

This ice was traditionally served during the winter months using reconstituted prickly pear before refrigeration became available. The dessert was left outside overnight to freeze and was enjoyed in the morning. Now the ice can be served any time of the year and is particularly refreshing in the hot summer months.

1 cup water
1½ teaspoons freshly squeezed lemon juice
½ cup sugar
2¾ cups prickly pear juice (page 118)
2 prickly pear cactus pads (nopales), scraped, trimmed
   (page 119), and cut into any shapes, for garnish

In a stainless steel or other nonreactive saucepan, bring the water and lemon juice to a boil over medium-high heat. Decrease the heat to low, add the sugar, and stir constantly until dissolved. Remove from the heat and stir in the prickly pear juice. Let cool.

Pour the liquid into a shallow glass or stainless-steel baking dish (do not use aluminum because the acid in the prickly pear juice will react with it) and place it in the freezer. Stir the liquid every 30 minutes until it has frozen into grainy, magenta-colored ice crystals. The process should take about 1½ hours, depending on the temperature of your freezer. You can also use an ice cream maker and freeze according to the manufacturer's directions.

Serve with the cactus pad garnish.

Serves 6

CACTUS PAD SALAD WITH FIERY JALAPEÑO DRESSING

On a warm summer day, nothing is more appetizing than a light, refreshing salad. In this one, the pleasing sweetness of oranges and the bell peppers balances the fiery flavor of the jalapeño dressing. The pumpkin seeds add a nice crunch.

CACTUS PAD SALAD

3 oranges

6 large prickly pear cactus pads (nopales), scraped, trimmed (see page 119), and cut into 3-inch strips

2 red bell peppers

¼ cup pumpkin seeds, lightly toasted

FIERY JALAPEÑO DRESSING

6 tablespoons sunflower oil

3 tablespoons tarragon vinegar or other herb-flavored vinegar

½ teaspoon salt

¼ teaspoon black pepper

½ teaspoon red chile powder

2 green jalapeño peppers, seeded and finely chopped

To make the salad, peel the oranges and cut into segments, removing the white pith.

Blanch the cactus pads in boiling salted water until they turn bright green, 1 to 2 minutes. Rinse thoroughly under cool water to remove their gum; drain well.

Roast, peel, and seed the red bell peppers using one of the methods described on pages 61–62. Cut into 3-inch strips.

In a bowl, toss together the oranges, cactus pad strips, red pepper strips, and pumpkin seeds.

To make the dressing, whisk together all of the ingredients. Pour the dressing over the salad, toss, and serve.

Serves 6

AZAFRÁN SOUP WITH SPINACH GREENS AND YELLOW CORNMEAL DUMPLINGS

Azafrán (Carthamus tinctorius) *are the stamens from the safflower. The safflower was introduced to New Mexico by the Spaniards as a substitute for true saffron. As well as adding it to recipes for flavor and color, many tribes historically used* azafrán *for medicinal purposes. Many Native Peoples as well as Spanish descendants still use* azafrán *medicinally, but the majority of people today use it as a spice in cooking. The subtle aromatic flavor of* azafrán *in this nutritious soup is wonderful with fresh, sweet vegetables. Serve this as a main course with Adobe Bread (page 68), Indian Frybread (page 68), or homemade tortillas (pages 33), or in smaller portions as an appetizer.*

YELLOW CORNMEAL DUMPLINGS

1 cup ground yellow cornmeal
¾ cup flour
2 teaspoons baking powder
1 teaspoon salt
½ teaspoon white pepper
2½ tablespoons sugar
1 teaspoon unsalted butter, softened
¾ cup milk
2 cups chicken stock (page 198)

AZAFRÁN SOUP

6 cups water
2 tablespoons azafrán (see note)
1 teaspoon salt
½ teaspoon white pepper
3 cups chicken stock (page 198)
2 yellow summer squash, diced
3 cups corn kernels (fresh, frozen, or canned)
1 bunch spinach greens, washed and stemmed

To make the dumplings, combine the cornmeal, flour, baking powder, salt, pepper, and sugar together in a bowl. Add the butter and milk and mix well to make a batter that is moist but not sticky. If the dough is too moist, knead in a little more flour. Divide the dough into 1-inch balls, flatten, and shape into small triangles or other shape.

Pour the chicken stock into a pot and bring to a boil over medium-high heat. Decrease the heat to a simmer and drop in the dumplings. Cook for 3 to 4 minutes, until tender and cooked all the way through. Remove the dumplings from the stock and set aside.

To make the soup, heat 2 cups of the water and the *azafrán* in a large saucepan over medium-high heat until the liquid has reduced by half, about 7 minutes. Pour through a fine sieve, discard the *azafrán,* and return the liquid to the saucepan. Add the salt, pepper, stock, and the remaining 4 cups of water and bring to a boil over medium-high heat. Add the squash, decrease the heat, and simmer for 5 minutes. Add the corn kernels and simmer for another 5 minutes. Add the dumplings and spinach, cook for 2 minutes, and serve immediately.
Serves 6

VARIATION: This dish can be made vegetarian by omitting the chicken stock and just using water. We tested it this way and it made a very nice vegetarian main course or appetizer.

NOTE: *Azafrán,* also called Native American saffron, is an herb that is actually the fine threads from the stigma of the safflower plant. Despite the name, *azafrán* is not the same as saffron, which is an expensive spice derived from the crocus plant in the iris family. (Saffron can be substituted for *azafrán,* though: use one pinch of saffron for 2 tablespoons of *azafrán.*)

Azafrán is commonly sold in Latin American markets, specialty herb stores, and gourmet cooking stores. It can also be ordered by mail (see Source Guide, page 201). It is best stored in a cool, dark place and will last several months in a sealed plastic or glass container.

PICURIS INDIAN BREAD PUDDING

Almost every Pueblo has their own version of bread pudding, and I have seen it served at every Feast Day I have ever attended. All are delicious (although I have never tasted a bread pudding recipe I didn't like). This recipe is from the Picuris Pueblo.

4 cups Adobe Bread Crumbs (page 68) or toasted
   crumbs from commercially bought bread
2 cups grated mild Cheddar cheese
1 teaspoon ground nutmeg
1 teaspoon ground cinnamon
2 cups sugar
4 cups water
4 tablespoons unsalted butter

Grease a 5 by 9-inch loaf pan with butter or lard and cover the bottom with 2 cups of the bread crumbs. Spread 1½ cups of the cheese over the bread crumbs. Sprinkle ½ teaspoon of the nutmeg, ½ teaspoon of the cinnamon, and ¼ cup of the sugar over the cheese.

Add the remaining 2 cups of the bread crumbs and pat down so the layers are firm. Make a second layer, using the remaining grated cheese, nutmeg, cinnamon, and ¼ cup of the sugar.

Heat the remaining 1½ cups sugar in a saucepan over medium heat, stirring occasionally until the sugar has melted. Add the water and let the sugar syrup dissolve. (Sometimes, when you add the water, the sugar syrup will harden, but it will melt again from the heat.) Add the butter and stir constantly until it has melted with the sugar syrup, 3 to 5 minutes. Pour over the layers in the loaf pan and test with a spoon to make sure the sugar syrup has saturated the bottom.

Preheat the oven to 300°. Bake the loaf for 30 to 40 minutes, until the cheese has browned and the sugar syrup is bubbling. Remove from the oven, place on a wire rack, and cool.

Cut into 1½-inch-thick slices and serve with Apricot Sauce (page 131), Peach Honey (page 131), or Prickly Pear Syrup (page 121). Use fresh apricots as a garnish if they are in season.

Serves 6 to 8

BIZCOCHITO COOKIES

These cookies, sometimes called Feast Day Cookies, are made in large batches and served at almost every Feast Day on all of the Pueblos throughout New Mexico. This is a traditional cookie that is also prepared by many of the families that are of Spanish descendant. Recipes may vary from household to household, but everyone recognizes these cookies because of the anise seeds in them.

1¾ cups sugar
1 cup unsalted butter
3 cups flour
1 teaspoon baking powder
2 teaspoons aniseed
2 eggs
½ teaspoon vanilla
½ teaspoon ground cinnamon

With a hand mixer or food processor, cream together 1½ cups of the sugar and the butter until well mixed. Sift together the flour and baking powder, then add the aniseed. Stir the dry ingredients in with the sugar and butter. Add the eggs and vanilla and mix well to make a smooth dough. Knead the dough on a floured board or work surface for 5 minutes. Form the dough into a ball and cover with plastic wrap. Place in the refrigerator and let chill for several hours or overnight.

Preheat the oven to 375°. Roll the dough out on a floured board or work surface to about ¼ inch thick. You may have to work it with your hands for several minutes after removing it from the refrigerator to soften it. Cut with a cookie cutter (any shapes can be used), and place them on a baking sheet lined with parchment paper or on a greased cookie sheet. Bake for 10 minutes or until golden brown. Remove from the oven and let cool. Combine the remaining ¼ cup sugar and the cinnamon. With a small strainer, dust the sugar-cinnamon mixture over each cookie. Place in a sealed container. These cookies will last for several days at room temperature.

Makes about 2 dozen cookies

Opposite: Bizcochito cookies pictured here with Prickly Pear and Indian Tea Ice.

NAVAJO PEACH PUDDING

Traditionally, only Indian peaches and water were used in this recipe. Although the simpler recipe is delicious, I have been taught this more modern variation, which I think you will enjoy.

½ cup honey
1 pound fresh peaches, peeled and pitted
1 cup water
1 package unflavored gelatin
1 cup heavy cream

In a food processor, purée the honey and peaches together. Set aside.

In a small saucepan, mix together the water and gelatin and let stand for 1 minute. Over medium-low heat, stir the mixture until the gelatin has completely dissolved, about 5 minutes. Remove from the heat, slowly add the gelatin mixture to the peach-honey purée, and blend thoroughly. Allow to cool to room temperature, about 5 minutes.

While the peach mixture is cooling, beat the cream until firm peaks have formed, about 2 minutes.

Fold the whipped cream into the peach pudding in a circular motion, leaving swirls of white cream in the peach pudding. Do not mix together completely.

Place the pudding in the refrigerator and chill until firm. Scoop out servings with a large spoon. If you prefer, you can place the peach pudding into individual cups, chill until firm, and then serve.
Serves 6

PEACH HONEY

Peach Honey can accompany a variety of dishes. I serve it with the Blue Cornmeal and Piñon Hotcakes (page 39), with the Feast Days Piñon Torte (page 157), and spread on Adobe Bread (page 68).

1 pound fresh, frozen, or dried peaches, peeled, pitted, and sliced (see note)
3 tablespoons honey
1 teaspoon freshly squeezed lemon juice

Blend all ingredients together in a food processor for 3 minutes to make a smooth purée. Pour into a squeeze bottle. The honey can be kept in the refrigerator for 1 to 2 weeks.
Makes 1 cup

NOTE: If using dried peaches, soak them in warm water to cover for 1½ hours, until soft and pliable. Remove the skins with your fingers, then proceed with the recipe, adding an extra tablespoon of honey, if necessary, to compensate for the tartness of the dried fruit. If using frozen peaches, follow the recipe as explained above.

APRICOT SAUCE

Apricots are seasonal, however, and canned or dried will also work. It is a great sauce with Picuris Indian Bread Pudding (page 126), with Blue Cornmeal and Piñon Hotcakes (page 39), or just spread over a warm piece of one of the Indian breads.

2 cups apple cider
½ cup sugar
18 fresh apricots, skinned, pitted, and quartered, or 2 16-ounce cans apricots, drained, or 1 cup dried apricots (see note)

Bring the apple cider to a boil in a saucepan over high heat. Add the sugar and stir constantly until the sugar has dissolved, about 1 minute. Add the apricots and again bring to a boil. Let boil for 30 minutes, stirring occasionally, until the apricots are soft and only a small amount of liquid is left on the bottom of the pan. If the consistency is too thick, add more apple cider.

Serve hot or place in the refrigerator to chill. The sauce will keep for 1 week in a covered container in the refrigerator.
Makes 3 cups

NOTE: Dried apricots must be reconstituted before cooking. Soak them overnight in a bowl with water to cover.

INDIAN TEA ICE (HOHOISE ICE)

During the spring and summer months of the high mesas of northern Arizona and throughout northern New Mexico, a yellow flowering wild herb called Indian tea, cota, or hohoise by the Hopis, grows in abundance. Cota (Thelesperma gracile) was widely used as a beverage before coffee or tea was introduced to this region. It still serves this purpose in the more isolated communities. For this recipe, some spices have been added to the tea to create a delicious ice that even children will enjoy.

1½ bundles Indian tea (hohoise) leaves and flowers
   (see note)
3 cups boiling water
¼ teaspoon ground cinnamon
1 cup sugar
½ teaspoon aniseed
2 cups water
6 star anise, for garnish
6 Indian tea flowers, for garnish

Add the bundles of Indian tea to the boiling water and continue to boil for 2 minutes over high heat. Remove from the heat and let steep for 10 minutes, covered. The liquid should turn a dark brown.

Add the cinnamon and sugar and mix well. Pour the liquid through a fine sieve or tea strainer to strain out the leaves and flowers. Set aside.

Mix together the aniseed and 2 cups water and let sit for 5 minutes. Pour through a fine sieve to remove the seeds.

Mix the tea and the anise liquid together. Pour into a shallow baking dish and place in the freezer. Stir the liquid every 30 minutes until it has frozen into grainy ice crystals. The process should take about 2 hours. You can also use an ice cream maker and freeze according to the manufacturer's directions.

Garnish with the star anise and Indian tea flowers.
Serves 6 as a dessert

NOTE: Indian tea can be obtained by mail order (see Source Guide, page 201). Otherwise, any herb tea, or even plain tea, can be substituted.

SUSTENANCE IN A POD

BEANS, NUTS, AND SEEDS

BECAUSE BEANS, nuts, and seeds were relatively easy to grow, gather, and store, they became important to the survival of the Native American people. They were—and are—a major part of the daily diet, providing high quantities of protein, carbohydrates, minerals, and vitamins. Special pottery urns and jars were used to store the harvest through winter and unproductive seasons. Beans and seeds were also traded and even offered as gifts.

Beans (*Phaseolus* spp.), along with squash (*Cucurbitas* spp.) and corn *(Zea mays)*, were domesticated in Mesoamerica between 7000 and 3000 B.C. Data from archaeological excavations in the Tehuacán Valley in central Mexico have supported this hypothesis.[i] Between 4800 and 3500 B.C., the common bean *(Phaseolus vulgaris)* was the first to be cultivated. By 3500 to 2300 B.C., jack beans *(Canavalia ensiformis)* and tepary beans *(Phaseolus acutifolius)* were being cultivated along with varieties of pumpkins and summer squashes.[ii] Common beans include types we recognize as pinto beans, red kidney beans, and navy beans. The common bean plant was eventually grown throughout the Southwest, and it may have been the only bean grown at some Pueblo sites.[iii]

It has often been noted, following Kaplan (1965), that corn and beans complement each other in two respects. First, beans contain a high level of the amino acid lysine, which enables efficient digestion of the protein available in corn. Second, whereas corn generally depletes nutrients from the soil, beans, as legumes, return nitrogen to the ground. When corn and beans are planted in the same field, problems of nutrient depletion are ameliorated.[iv] Because of this complementary relationship, it is surprising that beans appear later than corn in the archaeological record.[v]

Among the New World beans, there are many whose names, tastes, and uses are very well known. In addition to the pinto, kidney, and navy, the lima and wax are other worthy American beans. Still other beans are perhaps unappreciated outside of their own specific regions or ethnic groups, and some have slipped into relative obscurity.[vi]

Tepary beans have adapted to the Sonoran Desert and can be found throughout northwestern Mexico, Arizona, and New Mexico. Today, they are grown and eaten by the Akimiel O'odham (Pima), the Tohono O'odham (Papago), and some peoples of the lower Colorado River. Because of their high drought tolerance, teparies are perfect for growing in this arid region.

The main use of beans among Native Americans of the Southwest has always been as a dry, storable seed crop, with beans being harvested in the mature stage. Especially prized are white, blue, red, yellow, multicolored, and black beans, which symbolize the six cardinal points: East, West, South, North, Zenith, and Nadir, respectively. Today, it is believed that a number of old American varieties have been lost, some of them even in this century. Anthropological studies of traditional foods pinpoint disappearances of varieties from specific communities and locations. However, nonprofit organizations, such as Native Seeds/SEARCH, started by Gary Nabhan, are dedicated to preserving heirloom seed stocks and are working with Native communities throughout the Southwest to keep many of these indigenous strains available. This organization preserves and distributes the adapted and diverse varieties of agricultural seeds and their wild relatives and documents the educational role these seeds play in cultures of the American Southwest and northern Mexico. This is important not only for heirloom beans, but also for many other native crops of the Southwest.

Nuts have also been an important part of the Native diet in the Southwest. Wild piñons (Pinus edulis) can be found in the northern regions of both Arizona and New Mexico. Ancient Indian People were the custodians of a once vast piñon and juniper (Juniperus monosperma) "orchard" that provided them with materials for food, fuel, building, tools, and medicine.[vii] Few trees produce abundant seed crops every year, and the piñon is no exception. Cones and nuts do not mature until a year after flowering, and the nut fully develops in late August. A crop can be expected only about once every 6 years. These nuts contain more than 3,000 calories per pound, contain all twenty amino acids that make up complete protein, and must have constituted the most valuable wild plant food source for many prehistoric peoples living in the piñon-juniper ecozone.[viii] It is one of the most sought after wild plant foods by contemporary Pueblos and some of the tribes in Arizona, particularly the Diné (Navajo).

Acorns also played a very important part in the lives of Native Peoples. There are more than a dozen species of oaks (Quercus spp.) in Arizona and several species in the Rio Grande Pueblo Province, all of which have acorns. One of the most common, and the one I use for cooking in this book, is the Emory oak (Quercus emoryi), which grows primarily in Arizona and may be referred to as Black oak, or bellota in Spanish. The acorns are approximately ¾ inch long, with the lower third of the nut covered by a hairy cup. The Apache peoples originally lived in the region of this oak before they were relocated northeast to San Carlos. Many Apache women still keep a store of acorn meal on hand, and some collect more than 100 pounds of acorns a year. The nuts are gathered and eaten raw, ground into a meal, and sometimes roasted. Other tribes that savor this nut include the Akimiel O'odham (Pima), the Tohono O'odham (Papago), and the Diné (Navajo).

Other important wild nuts and beans include mesquite beans (Prosopis juliflora), which are utilized by the Indians of the Sonora Desert, and the black walnut (Juglans major), which are especially relished by the Apaches. The sunflower (Helianthus annuus) is also an important part of the Southwestern diet and grows in wild abundance throughout the Southwest. Sunflower seeds were traditionally gathered from wild growing plants and carefully ground and then tossed into the air using sifter baskets so that the hulls would blow away in the wind. The leftover kernels were then ground into a meal or used whole. Sunflower seeds were the Southwest's only domesticated food plant before the introduction of beans, corn, and squash. The plants needed little attention and grew rapidly in spite of weeds. Sunflower seeds are extremely nutritious and are a rich source of vitamin B_6. The seeds contain 50 percent oil, which is extracted by boiling. The oil is used for cooking and for grooming the hair. Today, sunflowers are grown in almost all Native American gardens along with corn, beans, squash, and melons. Roadsides, fields, and abandoned gardens are ideal habitats for this plant.

Beans, nuts, and seeds have been an important part of the Southwest for hundreds of years and continue to be so today.

ANASAZI AND PINTO BEANS WITH HOMINY AND GREEN CHILES

Most Southwestern Indians grow beans. The Hopis grow a variety of beans in terraces along their high mesas, where the crop is irrigated by natural springs. After the harvest, the beans are dried and stored. Some beans are used for ceremonial purposes—including wedding and Kachina dances—while others are used for day-to-day meals. To round out this meal, serve the beans with Lamb-stuffed Green Chiles (page 81), Pan-fried Trout (page 171), or Venison Steaks (page 189) and one of the many Indian breads, such as Piki Bread (page 51), Indian Frybread (page 68), or Adobe Bread (page 68).

1½ cups dried anasazi or appaloosa beans or other native beans (see note)
1½ cups pinto or other native beans
3 cups cooked Indian Hominy (page 29)
1 teaspoon salt
9 green New Mexico or Anaheim chiles, for garnish

Soak the anasazi and pinto beans overnight in water to cover. The next day, drain, rinse with cold water, and place in a large pot with fresh water to cover. Bring to a boil, then decrease the heat, cover, and simmer for 2 to 2½ hours, until the beans are tender. Add water when necessary and stir occasionally to prevent the beans from burning.

Add the hominy and salt, and simmer, covered, for 1 hour, stirring occasionally. The hominy and beans should be soft and moist but not too watery.

While the beans and hominy are cooking, roast, peel, seed, and dice the chiles (page 61). Sprinkle on top of the cooked beans and serve.

Serves 6 to 8

NOTE: The appaloosa is a gracefully slender, curved oval bean with mottled purple-white marking and is a classic heirloom bean. The bean is the same as the anasazi, named for the civilization that flourished over 1,000 years ago in New Mexico, Arizona, Utah, and Colorado. Anasazi, Diné (Navajo) for "the ancient ones," is the name given to the Native Peoples who created the cliff dwellings in the Southwest. The sweet-tasting anasazi bean is one of the first foods cultivated by the Native Americans. It is high in protein, holds its shape when it cooks, and delivers a richly piney, herbaceous flavor. The color mellows as it cooks to a pink and burgundy color.

For suburban and city dwellers, I've found that pinto beans, white beans, or red beans also work well in this recipe, but I suggest you experiment with some of the other varieties of beans, such as anasazi, tepary, or some of the Native heirloom varieties (see Source Guide, page 201) that are now available commercially. Native Seeds/SEARCH is a nonprofit conservation organization that sells many indigenous beans by the pound and as seeds. You may want to be adventuresome and grow some of these native seed varieties to begin your own personal seed bank for future plantings.

PINON CHILE BEANS

This recipe comes from the Begay family on the Diné (Navajo) reservation in Pinon, Arizona. It is their favorite chile bean recipe and I am asked to cook it every time I visit. This recipe is so great because you can make one recipe to feed six to eight people or you can multiply it and make enough to feed sixty people. It is a favorite at all family and ceremonial gatherings. This recipe goes great with warm Indian Frybread or Adobe Bread (page 68). It makes a hearty meal by itself or as a side to any feast.

2 tablespoons olive oil
1 large yellow onion, chopped
2 green bell peppers, seeded, deveined, and chopped
2 pounds lean ground beef
1 (28-ounce) can whole peeled tomatoes with basil
2½ cups cooked dark red kidney beans
2½ cups cooked pinto beans
2 cups cooked corn kernels (fresh, frozen, or canned)
3 tablespoons red chile powder
1 teaspoon salt

Heat the oil in a large cast-iron or soup pot over medium-high heat. Add the onions, sauté for 2 minutes, until translucent, then add the green bell peppers and sauté for another 2 to 4 minutes. Add the ground beef, stir, and sauté until the meat is brown, 7 to 10 minutes.

Cut each of the whole tomatoes into eight pieces (a large dice) and add the pieces to the meat, onions, and peppers. Cook for another 2 minutes, stirring constantly. Add the kidney beans, pinto beans, and the corn and stir well. Bring to a boil, then decrease the heat to low. Stir in the red chile powder and salt. Let simmer for 20 minutes, stirring occasionally to prevent burning. Serve hot. *Serves 6 to 8*

INDIAN TACOS (TRADITIONAL VERSION)

1 cup dried pinto beans
4 green New Mexico or Anaheim chiles
1 tablespoon olive oil
1 onion, coarsely chopped
1 pound lean ground beef
1 teaspoon salt
6 pieces Indian Frybread (page 68)
2 cups lettuce, shredded
2 tomatoes, diced
2 cups grated Cheddar cheese

The Indian Taco has become one of today's best-known Native American dishes. It is served at national fairs, intertribal pow-wows, and community events, both on the reservations and in urban areas. Its base, unlike the more familiar Mexican-style taco, is a piece of frybread, made from a light dough and considered to be of Diné (Navajo) origin. This bread used to be fried in lard, but now more and more people are using vegetable shortening or oil for frying. Indian Tacos are relatively easy to prepare and make a wonderful lunch or dinner.

To prepare the pinto beans, soak them overnight in water to cover. The next day, drain the beans and place them in a saucepan with fresh water to cover. Bring to a boil, decrease the heat, and let the beans simmer until the skins break and the beans are soft, about 3 hours. It may be necessary to add water as the beans cook to prevent them from burning and sticking. After the beans are cooked, remove from the heat and set aside. You should have about 2 cups of cooked beans.

While the beans are cooking roast, peel, seed and devein the chiles (page 61), and then chop them.

In a skillet over medium-high heat, add the oil and sauté the onion for 3 minutes until translucent, then add the ground beef and cook for another 5 to 6 minutes, until the meat has browned. Pour off any fat. Add the beans, chiles, and salt and decrease heat and cook for another 5 minutes. Remove from the heat and set aside.

Make the frybread according to the recipe on page 68 and set aside.

Reheat the meat, bean, and chile mixture so that it is warm and begin building your tacos. Place some of the meat, bean, and chile mixture, about 1 cup, on top of each piece of frybread. Place some lettuce, diced tomatoes, and grated cheese on top of the meat, bean, and chile mixture. Serve immediately.
Serves 6

INDIAN TACOS (MODERN VERSION)

This version of the Indian Taco includes ingredients that you will not see in the traditional version, except for its frybread base (page 68). This recipe also includes anasazi beans (see note, page 139) instead of the traditional pinto beans. The anasazi bean is related to the pinto bean, however, and if you cannot find these beans, you can substitute pintos. For many years, this bean was seldom used and hard to find, but it is gaining popularity in the commercial market. It can be found in health-food stores and can be ordered by mail (see Source Guide, page 201).

1½ cups dried anasazi beans
6 green New Mexico or Anaheim chiles
1 large red bell pepper
6 pieces Indian Frybread (page 68)
1½ cups mâche or arugula, washed and stemmed
1 large ripe red tomato, sliced
2 ripe avocados, halved and sliced
1 red onion, thinly sliced
1 bunch red radishes, sliced
18 golden yellow plum tomatoes, halved

To prepare the anasazi beans, soak them overnight in water to cover. The next day, drain the beans and place them in a saucepan with fresh water to cover. Bring to a boil, decrease the heat, and let the beans simmer until the skins break and the beans are soft, about 3 hours. It may be necessary to add water as the beans cook to prevent them from burning and sticking. After the beans are cooked, remove from the heat and set aside. You should have about 3 cups of cooked beans.

While the beans are cooking, roast, seed, and devein the chiles and the red bell pepper (page 61). Leave the green chiles whole; slice the red bell pepper lengthwise into small strips.

Make the frybread according to the recipe and set aside.

Reheat the beans so that they are warm and begin building your tacos. Place ½ cup cooked beans on each piece of frybread. For each taco, add ¼ cup mâche, followed by a red tomato slice; add 4 slices avocado and 1 slice red onion separated into rings; follow with radish slices and 6 golden yellow plum tomato halves; and top with 1 roasted green chile and 2 slices roasted red bell pepper.

You can vary the toppings and the order in which the taco is built. Serve immediately.

Serves 6

Opposite: Calandra Willie, Diné (Navajo) in traditional dress.

GARBANZO BEAN STEW

Margaret Archuleta of Picuris Pueblo taught me the recipe for this simple and satisfying stew made with garbanzo beans. I first tasted it while celebrating New Year's Day with her family. The only difference here is that I brown the meat before adding it to the garbanzo beans.

2 pounds dried garbanzo beans
10 cups water
1½ tablespoons olive oil
1 onion, chopped
2 cloves garlic, finely chopped
2 pounds stew beef or venison, cut into 1-inch cubes
4 cups veal stock (page 200)
1 teaspoon salt
½ teaspoon white pepper

Soak the garbanzo beans overnight in twice their volume of water. The beans will absorb much of the water and swell in size. The following day, drain and rinse the beans under cold running water. Place the beans in a large pot with the 10 cups of water. Bring to a boil over high heat, decrease the heat to low, and simmer, uncovered, 1½ hours, stirring occasionally to prevent burning.

In a sauté pan, heat the olive oil over medium heat and add the onion. Sauté for 1 to 2 minutes, until the onion is translucent, then add the garlic. Cook for 1 minute, then add the meat and sauté for 2 minutes on each side, until browned. Remove from the heat.

Add the sautéed meat, veal stock, salt, and pepper to the beans and continue cooking for another 2 hours, until the meat is tender and the beans are fully cooked.

Serve hot with one of the many Indian breads, such as Indian Tortillas (page 33), Adobe Bread (page 68), or *Piki* Bread (page 51).
Serves 6 to 8

INDIAN BEAN TERRINE IN BROWN HERB SAUCE WITH BLUE CORNMEAL TORTILLA FEATHERS

This hearty terrine can be served either as an appetizer or as a main course accompanied by a salad. Because the terrine is a bit time-consuming to prepare, I usually make it a day in advance and reheat it just before serving. This enhances the flavor of the dish and allows the terrine to set fully.

INDIAN BEAN TERRINE

1 pound dried small white or pinto beans
1 tablespoon unsalted butter, softened
½ cup yellow cornmeal
2 cups water or reserved liquid from soaking the beans
1 tablespoon salt
⅛ teaspoon white pepper
1 tablespoon red chile powder
1 tablespoon ground cumin

BROWN HERB SAUCE

3 cups veal stock (page 200)
4 tablespoons unsalted butter, softened
2 tablespoons chopped fresh tarragon
3 tablespoons chopped fresh chives
2 tablespoons chopped fresh dill
2 tablespoons chopped fresh basil

BLUE CORNMEAL TORTILLA FEATHERS

8 Blue Cornmeal Tortillas (page 33)
1 cup vegetable oil

8 whole chives, for garnish
32 sprigs chervil, for garnish

To make the bean terrine, soak the beans overnight in water to cover. The next day, drain the beans, rinse with cold water, and place in a pot with fresh water to cover. Bring to a boil over high heat, then decrease the heat and simmer for several hours, until the beans are soft. Remove from the heat and drain. Mash the beans and mix with the softened butter and cornmeal. (You can mash the beans in a food processor, which is the easiest method, or by hand with a potato masher.) Set aside.

Bring the 2 cups of water to a boil over high heat. Add the bean mixture, salt, pepper, red chile powder, and cumin. Decrease the heat and simmer for 20 minutes, stirring constantly to prevent burning. Pour into a greased 5 by 9-inch loaf pan, cool to room temperature, and chill in the refrigerator overnight or until firm. (I have found that if you line the greased loaf pan with plastic wrap before placing the bean mixture into it, it is easier to get the bean terrine out.) Unmold the bean terrine from the loaf pan, cut into about ½-inch slices, and set on a cookie sheet. Reheat in a preheated 350° oven for 10 minutes, until warm.

To make the herb sauce, bring the stock to a boil in a large saucepan over moderate heat. Add the butter and stir until completely melted. Add the tarragon, chives, dill, and basil. Stir for 1 minute and remove from the heat.

To make the tortilla feathers, cut the tortillas into feather shapes with scissors or a small paring knife. In a skillet over moderate to high heat, heat the oil until it almost reaches the smoking point. Using tongs, dip each tortilla feather into the hot oil, remove, and blot dry with a paper towel.

Spoon some herb sauce onto each plate and place two slices of the warm bean terrine in the center. Garnish each with a tortilla feather, a whole chive, and sprigs of chervil.

Serves 8

SPICY PINTO BEAN RAVIOLI WITH CORN AND CHILE CREAM SAUCE

This recipe combines many simple ingredients commonly used in Native American cooking. Although ravioli are quite familiar to most people, these are made from blue cornmeal. They are filled with a zesty bean purée flavored with several herbs and red chile powder.

SPICY PINTO BEAN RAVIOLI

2 cups dried pinto beans

1 teaspoon dried oregano

1 teaspoon ground cumin

4 cloves garlic, unpeeled

1 small onion, chopped

¼ cup vegetable oil

1 tablespoon red chile powder

1 teaspoon salt

1 recipe Blue Cornmeal Ravioli Dough
   (see variation, page 152)

1 egg, beaten, for egg wash

CORN AND CHILE CREAM SAUCE

6 green New Mexico or Anaheim chiles

4 cups corn kernels (fresh, frozen, or canned)

3 serrano chiles, seeded and chopped

1 teaspoon salt

½ teaspoon white pepper

2 cups heavy cream

Red chiles, for garnish
Green chiles, for garnish

To make the ravioli, soak the beans overnight in water to cover. The next day, drain, rinse with cold water, and place them in a saucepan with fresh water to cover. Bring to a boil over high heat, then decrease the heat and simmer for several hours, until the beans become soft and the skins begin to split. Add water when necessary and stir occasionally to prevent the beans from burning. Remove from the heat.

Toast the oregano and cumin in a dry sauté pan over medium heat until lightly browned. Remove from the pan and set aside. Add the unpeeled garlic to the pan and roast over medium heat until it is soft and blackened in spots. Let cool, then peel and mash with a knife.

In a saucepan, sauté the onion in 1 tablespoon of the oil over moderate heat until it is lightly browned. Decrease the heat to low, add the mashed garlic, and cook for 1 minute. Add the oregano, cumin, red chile powder, salt, beans, and just enough water to cover, about 2 to 3 cups. Bring to a boil over high heat, then decrease the heat and simmer, uncovered, 30 minutes.

Purée the bean mixture in a food processor until it is smooth.

In a cast iron skillet, heat the remaining oil over high heat to its smoking point. Add the bean purée and stir for 1 minute. Decrease the heat to moderate and cook for 5 minutes, while stirring, until the bean purée is a medium paste. It will thicken as it cools.

Next, prepare the ravioli dough following the directions. Divide the dough in half and roll out each portion of the dough into a rectangle, 12 by 15 inches and ⅛ inch thick. With the back of a knife, lightly mark 3-inch squares on the dough. With a basting brush, spread a thin layer of egg wash, about 1 inch wide, along the marked lines on the dough. Place 1 tablespoon of bean filling in the center of each square with a spoon.

recipe continues on following page

Roll out the remaining dough to the same size as the bottom layer and place on top. With your fingers press down around each mound of filling to release the air and seal each piece of ravioli. Cut between the mounds with a pasta crimper and sealer, making sure the top and bottom layers of the pasta dough are sealed securely. Set on a baking pan or tray dusted with flour so the ravioli don't stick and set aside while you make the sauce. Ravioli can be frozen for later use at this point if you wish.

To make the cream sauce, roast the green chiles (page 61), then peel, seed, devein, and dice them. Combine 3 cups of the corn, ⅔ of the diced green chiles, the serrano chiles, salt, and pepper in a food processor and process for about 2 minutes, until smooth. Scrape the sides and process for another 30 seconds. Push through a fine sieve and discard the skins.

Put the mixture in a saucepan and heat over moderate heat for 3 minutes, slowly adding the cream while stirring. Add the remaining corn kernels and diced green chiles. Decrease the heat to low and simmer for 5 minutes, until the corn is tender. Set aside to keep warm.

Fill a large pot with water and bring to a boil. Place the ravioli in the water and cook for 3 to 5 minutes (see note), until tender.

Drain the ravioli and serve immediately with the cream sauce. Allow 2 to 3 ravioli per person. Garnish with the red and green chiles.
Serves 6 as an appetizer

NOTE: Cooking ravioli above sea level requires a longer cooking time. Add 1 minute of cooking time for every 1,000 feet above sea level.

BASIC EGG RAVIOLI DOUGH

Walter Whitewater, a contemporary Native American chef, makes fresh dough on a regular basis. He believes his dough is so good because of his intent when he makes it. He believes that whatever you are thinking when you make the dough goes into the dough through your hands. This is why Native cooks always tell you never to make dough when you are angry or have negative thoughts.

This basic dough makes excellent ravioli, which can be stuffed with a variety of ingredients and used for appetizers, soups, and main courses.

3 cups sifted flour
4 eggs
1 teaspoon salt
1 teaspoon vegetable oil

Pour the flour into a mound on a flat work surface. With your hand, make a depression in the center that almost reaches through to the board. Crack the eggs directly into the well and, with a fork, whip in the salt and oil, mixing the flour in from around the edges.

Mix and knead the dough with your hands for 8 to 10 minutes, until the dough has a smooth and elastic consistency. If the dough seems a bit dry, add a little more water; add a little more flour if it seems too moist. Once you have obtained the desired consistency, cover the dough with plastic wrap and place it in the refrigerator for 15 minutes.

Divide the dough into handfuls and roll out each section very thin, until it is almost translucent.

Use your imagination to cut the dough into any size or shape. Any filling can be used to make the ravioli.
Makes 12 large or 24 small raviolis

VARIATION: To make blue cornmeal ravioli, substitute a combination of 1 cup finely ground blue cornmeal and 1½ cups flour for the flour in this recipe. Increase the number of eggs to five.

ACORN RAVIOLI IN CLEAR BROTH

During my travels throughout the southern Apache lands of Arizona, I was introduced to the acorns of the Emory oak (Quercus emoryi) and taught how to gather and harvest them. Found from southeastern to central Arizona, the acorns of this species of oak are much lower in tannic acid than acorns of other oaks, need no leaching, and can be eaten as the nuts fall to the ground. When working with acorns in your kitchen, place them on a flat wood surface and firmly press the flat side of a large knife (as you would garlic) on top of the nuts to break them open. Then, simply peel the shells away and use according to the recipe.

ACORN RAVIOLI

4 green New Mexico or Anaheim chiles

2 tablespoons unsalted butter

3 tablespoons shelled and finely chopped acorns or
   unsalted pistachio nuts

8 to 10 ounces (about 1 cup) soft white goat cheese

1 recipe Basic Egg Ravioli Dough (opposite page)

1 egg, beaten, for egg wash

2 teaspoons kosher salt

1 teaspoon vegetable oil

1 quart water

CLEAR BROTH

6 cups chicken stock (page 198) or rabbit stock
   (page 199)

¼ cup scallions, green part only, sliced diagonally

1 teaspoon *azafrán* (see note, page 125)

½ teaspoon salt

To make the ravioli, roast the chiles (see page 61), then peel, seed, devein, and coarsely chop them. Melt the butter in a saucepan over medium-low heat and add the acorns. Sauté for 3 minutes, stirring constantly. Add the green chiles and sauté for 1 minute. Remove from the heat, mix together with the goat cheese, and set aside.

Next, prepare the ravioli dough following the directions. Roll out the ravioli dough as thinly as possible. (I usually use setting number six on a pasta maker.) Fold the dough in half and roll out each portion of the dough into a square, 15 by 15 inches. With the back of a knife, lightly mark 3-inch squares on the dough. You should have 25 ravioli marked. With a basting brush, spread a thin layer of egg wash, about 1 inch wide, along the marked lines on the dough. Place 1 full teaspoon of the chile filling into the center of each square with a spoon.

Roll out the remaining dough to the same size as the bottom layer and place on top. With your fingers press down around each mound of filling to release the air and seal each piece of ravioli. Cut between the mounds with a pasta crimper and sealer, making sure the top and bottom layers of the pasta dough are securely sealed. Set on a baking pan or tray dusted with flour so the ravioli don't stick and set aside while you make the broth. Ravioli can be frozen for later use at this point if you wish.

To make the broth, bring the stock to a boil in a large saucepan over medium-high heat. Add the scallions, *azafrán,* and salt and simmer, uncovered, over medium-low heat for 5 minutes.

Add the kosher salt and oil to the water in a wide, large saucepan and bring to a boil over high heat. Add the ravioli and cook 3 minutes (see note), until tender and translucent around the edges.

Drain and set aside.

Pour 1 cup of the broth into each bowl. Add some ravioli and serve.

Serves 6 as an appetizer

NOTE: Cooking ravioli above sea level requires a longer cooking time. Add 1 minute of cooking time for every 1,000 feet above sea level.

ACORN-PIÑON SOUP WITH WILD FLOWERS

Traditionally, this recipe is prepared with the small, brown acorns of the Emory oak (Quercus emoryi), *which is indigenous to the Chiricahua Mountains in the southeastern part of Arizona. All oaks have acorns, but unlike those of other regions, the southwestern species are sweet just as they come off the tree or shrub, have very little tannin, and need no leaching or other preparation before eating.*

1 tablespoon unsalted butter
1 cup piñons (pine nuts)
4 tablespoons chopped shelled acorns or unsalted
   pistachio nuts
6 tablespoons chopped wild onion (see note, page 87)
   or leeks, white and green parts
9 cups chicken stock (page 198)
½ teaspoon salt
¼ teaspoon black pepper
1½ quarts half-and-half
Snipped wild onions, mint sprigs, and wild edible
   flowers, for garnish

Melt the butter in a large saucepan over medium heat and sauté the piñons, acorns, and onions for 4 minutes, until the onions are translucent and the nuts golden brown.

Add the stock, salt, and pepper. Bring to a boil, then decrease the heat to medium, and cook until the mixture is reduced by half, about 20 minutes. Add the half-and-half and reduce the mixture again by half, to about 6 cups.

Remove from the heat and blend in a blender or food processor until the mixture is smooth. Push through a fine sieve; discard the contents of the sieve. Garnish with the wild onions, mint, and edible flowers and serve.
Serves 6

Above: Charlotte S. Titla (San Carlos Apache) gathering acorns.

FEAST DAYS PIÑON TORTE

The Feast Day is one of the biggest celebrations of the year among the Indian Pueblos of New Mexico. To honor their Patron Saints, the people of each Pueblo gather together. They attend mass in the morning and hold a procession to the plaza where an altar houses their Patron Saint. After mass, many of the women return home to prepare the day's Feast, including a variety of salads, stews, meats, homemade breads, and, of course, desserts—traditional as well as modern dishes. People drop in throughout the day to taste the fine foods at many different houses. It is a festive day filled with warmth and friendliness. This recipe is my adaptation of some of the tortes I sampled at different Pueblos.

1 cup piñons (pine nuts)
2 tablespoons cornmeal
2 tablespoons unsalted butter
9 ounces semisweet chocolate
6 egg yolks
¾ cup granulated sugar
1 teaspoon vanilla extract
¼ cup confectioners' sugar and 2 tablespoons blue
    cornmeal, for decoration (optional)

Grease and flour a 9-inch round cake pan. Preheat the oven to 350°.

In a food processor, grind the piñons to a moist nutmeal. Add the cornmeal and blend again for about 30 seconds, just long enough to combine.

In a double boiler over medium-high heat, melt the butter and chocolate together, stirring occasionally so that they melt and blend together evenly. Add to the piñon mixture in the food processor and blend for about 1 minute until smooth.

Beat the egg yolks, granulated sugar, and vanilla together in a bowl, and add to the other ingredients in the food processor. Blend again until smooth.

Pour the batter into the prepared pan and pat down with your fingers until evenly spread (this is a thick batter). Bake 20 minutes, or until the cake is firm and springs back when the center is touched. This is a dense torte and resembles dense brownies. Remove from the oven and place on a wire rack to cool before decorating.

When the torte has cooled, after 20 to 30 minutes, remove it from the pan and decorate creatively. You can do individual stencils on each slice or decorate the entire torte. To make the southwestern motif pictured, cut a stencil out of cardboard. First dust the cake with confectioners' sugar using a medium sieve, lightly tapping the sides and moving it in a circular motion around the surface of the torte. Then, carefully holding the stencil as close to the torte's surface as possible without touching it, sprinkle the blue cornmeal through a sieve over the exposed areas. Carefully remove the stencil without disrupting the design. For a finishing touch, place a few piñons at the corner of each stenciled triangle.

Serves 6 to 8

Above: Traditional dancers (Picuris Pueblo) honoring their Patron Saint, San Lorenzo, at their Feast Day.

ZUNI SUNFLOWER CAKES

Many of the tribes and Pueblos throughout the Southwest grow sunflowers. The most common of these is the annual sunflower (Helianthus annuus), *which grows wild in open, undisturbed areas where there is a little extra water available. These plants need very little care, grow fairly quickly, and produce a nutritious seed that is delicious when ground. Sunflower seeds, rich in vitamins, minerals, and oils, have been used widely by Indians for centuries, parched and eaten whole or ground into flour. Seeds put through a grinder can be mixed with flour or cornmeal for mush, bread making, soups, and stews and can be made into cakes. Whether they are raw, roasted, or ground, sunflower seeds are a delicious addition to many recipes. Sunflower cakes make an excellent breakfast dish or can be eaten as a snack anytime.*

3 cups shelled sunflower seeds
3 cups water
5 tablespoons finely ground blue cornmeal
1 tablespoon sugar
½ cup vegetable oil

Combine the sunflower seeds and water in a saucepan and bring to a boil over high heat. Reduce the heat and simmer, uncovered, 15 minutes, until almost all of the water has evaporated.

Remove from the heat and drain the excess water from the seeds. Place the seeds in a food processor. Add the blue cornmeal and sugar and process 3 minutes, until the seeds are completely ground. If there are still whole seeds around the edges of the food processor, scrape them into the center with a spatula and process again until they are ground, about 1 minute more. The dough will be quite thick.

With your hands, shape the dough into round cakes about the size of silver dollars.

In a large skillet, heat the oil until it is hot but not smoking. Place the cakes in the pan and brown them for 2 to 3 minutes on each side, turning once. Remove from the oil and pat dry with paper towels.

Serve warm with Apricot Sauce (page 131), Peach Honey (page 131), Fresh Herb Jelly (page 111), or Chile Pepper Jelly (page 77).
Serves 6

Opposite: Sunflower cakes with herb jelly (top). Tiffany Georgeina Morgan with a sunflower in her grandmother's garden (bottom).

THE LAND'S CREATURES

GAME BIRDS, MEATS, AND FISH

THROUGHOUT HISTORY, Native Americans have been known for their ability to live solely off what the land provides. Cultivators and harvesters of many foods, they are also skilled hunters of game. They treat the land and the land's creatures with respect and gratitude. The traditional hunter never hunted for sport but killed only what was needed for survival. This respect for the natural balance of things is a basic Native American creed. All parts of the animal were used: meat for eating, skins for clothing, sinew for sewing and fastening, bones for tools, and hooves for ceremonial rattles.

In some tribes, before a hunter goes out in pursuit of game, he prays that an animal be provided for him so he can nourish himself and his family. In some cases, he makes an offering to the spirit of the animal. There exists a belief that when one hunts game meat, he is not only feeding his family but also sharing a oneness with the spirit of the animal. Today, game is hunted with the same spirit among most Native Americans.

Traditionally, the three most common Southwestern game animals were the mule deer, pronghorn antelope, and Rocky Mountain bighorn sheep. Mule deer have been known to live throughout the environments of the Southwest and have been encountered among the paloverde and cactus shrubland of the American Desert province, although they are more likely to be found in the piñon-juniper woodlands and in the southern Rocky Mountains. Bighorn sheep are rare today, except where herds have been reintroduced and are protected.

White-tailed deer occur in the Chihuahuan Desert, although their numbers are not as great as those of the mule deer. Elk are of local importance on the Colorado plateaus, in the southern Rocky Mountains, and in the Upper Gila Mountains, although it is believed that they had a more extensive range in the past. Elk meat is traditionally dried into jerky, and the Southern Ute women still dry elk on a regular basis. Bison (buffalo) require extensive grasslands, and they were found primarily in the easternmost margins of the Southwest.[i] Tribes here in the Southwest traded for bison meat with tribes from the plains. Today, some of the northern Pueblos have begun tending herds of buffalo on their own.

Smaller animals account for the remainder of animals that are hunted. Jackrabbits and cottontails proliferate throughout the Southwest and are hunted today, although not as extensively as in the past. Various birds are important to contemporary peoples. Turkeys were domesticated prehistorically in the Southwest by some groups and were used for their feathers as well as their meat. Wild birds commonly hunted for food have included quail, dove, squab, and robin. Quail and dove are the most popular and are still hunted today. Fish, including catfish and trout, are used regularly today. Trout is the more popular of the two presently.

Today, hunting has more of a ceremonial and spiritual purpose. Many of these wild game animals remain alive in the Winter Animal Dances of the many Pueblo tribes. Deer, antelope, and mountain sheep are honored by these dances. Ceremonial dancers wear antlers, animal skins, and evergreen branches representing the animals in their forest environment. To ensure that the ancient hunting methods are preserved for the generations to come, children are taught to use the bow and arrow, still an integral part of some ceremonial dances.

Now, hunting has restrictions. Permits are required in most areas, and the hunting of some species is prohibited except in certain seasons. Throughout the Southwest, however, hunting is still practiced, using both traditional and modern techniques. Consult an experienced hunter or guide before attempting to hunt on your own. It is also important to know that rabbits can carry disease, as do other types of wild game, and they should only be killed and dressed by experienced hunters.

Each region of the Southwest has different varieties of game birds, meats, and fish. Game birds are abundant in the desert and higher altitudes of the forest regions. They are commonly hunted and are frequently used in Native American recipes. Jackrabbits and cottontails are commonly seen throughout the majority of the Southwest and are also featured in some traditional

recipes. In most states, domestic game birds and meats are available from meat markets and breeders.

With the introduction of the horse, sheep, goat, cattle, and pig, among other things, in the early 1600s by the Spanish, life changed not only for the Pueblo People but also the Diné (Navajo). Traditional meat diets changed in the Southwest. By the 1700s, many Diné relied less on hunting and adopted a life of herding sheep. From the time the Diné first acquired sheep, their flocks have been central to their culture. A large number of traditional Diné continue to this day to herd sheep and cattle, using the sheep and cattle meat for food and the wool for weaving. The Diné have become master weavers, their blankets sometimes telling stories of a family's past or present. Sheep were—and still are—a sign of wealth and stability in a Diné family. They are given as a dowry to a young girl's family from her prospective husband.

The Apache engaged in subsistence farming, but their economy was based primarily on the exploitation of a wide variety of natural resources by hunting and gathering. Approximately 75 percent of their traditional diet was a combination of meat and undomesticated plants. Not relying on crops throughout the year, the western Apache did not establish permanent residences. Except for the planting in early spring and the harvest in the early fall, they were almost constantly on the move. Hunting was best in the late fall, and once a good supply of game was secured, the people would move again to their winter camps, completing their annual cycle.[ii] Today, some groups of Apaches still have hunts.

Many Pueblos are located along the Rio Grande, and in some of the smaller rivers and streams there is an abundance of fish, primarily trout. It took great patience to catch fish using the ancient methods first devised by the Native Americans. Today, the old ways are still taught, but modern methods are more commonly used.

The Southwest, with its vast stretches of land and varied terrain, is surprisingly filled with life. Hunting has always been a part of life here and continues to be today. Animals are hunted for food but are also honored and revered in the dances from the many different Pueblos and tribes living in the Southwest today.

APACHE STEW

This stew is based on a traditional stew that I was taught on the Apache reservation in San Carlos. I was told that the stew was always made after a deer hunt and that the ingredients varied each time the stew was prepared depending on what type of produce is available. Many traditional Native American stews were cooked with the meat still on the bones, creating its own flavorful stock as it cooked. Here, I have substituted veal stock and cubed venison. If you make this from deer meat that you have received from a hunt, however, leave it on the bones, follow the directions as listed below (with the exception of substituting water for stock), and cook longer until the meat is tender.

2 red bell peppers
4 green New Mexico or Anaheim chiles
¼ cup sunflower oil
1 pound venison, cut into 1½-inch cubes
1 onion, diced
3 cloves garlic, finely chopped
2 carrots, peeled and sliced
3 cups cooked Indian Hominy (page 29)
4 cups water
4 cups veal stock (page 200)
1½ teaspoons salt
½ teaspoon white pepper
1 cup bitter greens, such as curly endive or
    tumbleweed greens (see page 113), thoroughly
    cleaned and coarsely chopped

Roast the red bell peppers and green chiles (page 61), then peel, seed, devein, and dice.

Heat the oil in a large stew pot over medium-high heat. When the oil is almost smoking, add the venison and cook until the meat is lightly browned, about 3 to 5 minutes. Add the onion and garlic and sauté for 2 minutes more.

Stir in the carrots, red bell peppers, and green chiles and cook for another 2 minutes. Add the hominy, water, stock, salt, and pepper and bring to a boil. Decrease the heat to low and let the stew simmer for 1½ hours, stirring occasionally to avoid burning, until the meat is very tender. Just before serving, add the bitter greens, stir 1 minute, and spoon into bowls.
Serves 8 to 10

STUFFED QUAIL WITH SQUAWBERRY SAUCE

Squawberries (Rhus trilobata), also called lemonade berries, are bright red berries coated with a hairy stickiness and have a pleasantly acidic, lemony taste. Many Tewa Indians eat squawberries whole or ground. Relief from thirst has been found by sucking these acidic berries, which stimulate the flow of saliva, and many people make a refreshing beverage from the fruit, particularly welcome during the heat of summer days. Here, the tart flavor of squawberries is infused into a sauce. You can substitute pink peppercorns and lemon juice if the berries are unavailable to you.

STUFFED QUAIL

6 quail, backbones removed
2½ teaspoons salt
2¼ teaspoons black pepper
2 tablespoons olive oil
½ cup corn kernels (fresh, frozen, or canned)
1 cup White Sage Bread Crumbs (page 68)
½ cups shelled black walnuts, very finely chopped
1 tablespoon chopped fresh chives
1 tablespoon chopped fresh sage leaves
⅓ cup veal stock (page 200)
6 tablespoons unsalted butter, melted

SQUAWBERRY SAUCE

2 cups cold water
⅓ cup squawberries or pink peppercorns (see note)
2 teaspoons freshly squeezed lemon juice (only if using pink peppercorns)
3 cups veal stock (page 200)
8 tablespoons unsalted butter

Whole sage leaves, for garnish

To make the stuffed quail, wash each quail under cold water and season with 2 teaspoons salt and 2 teaspoons pepper.

For the stuffing, heat the oil in a saucepan and sauté the corn for 2 minutes, stirring constantly. Add the bread crumbs, walnuts, herbs, ½ teaspoon salt, and ¼ teaspoon pepper in a bowl. Stir in the stock and 3 tablespoons of the melted butter.

Generously stuff each quail cavity and place in a glass baking dish. Set aside.

To make the sauce, put the water and squawberries in a blender and process for 3 minutes. Strain the liquid through a fine sieve or cheesecloth into a saucepan; squeeze out as much liquid as possible and discard the solids.

Bring the liquid to a boil, then decrease the heat and simmer for 10 minutes. Add the stock and butter and continue simmering until the sauce has reduced by about one third, about 15 minutes. Remove from the heat and set aside.

Preheat the oven to 350°.

Baste the quail with some of the remaining melted butter, spoon some of the sauce over the quail, and place the dish in the oven. Bake for 40 minutes, basting with the remaining melted butter every 5 minutes.

Gently reheat the reserved sauce. Serve the quail dressed with sauce and garnish with sage leaves.

Serves 6

NOTES: Pink peppercorns do not taste as tart as squawberries and they have a faint taste of pepper to them. If substituting peppercorns for squawberries, add 1 teaspoon of freshly squeezed lemon juice for each ¼ cup of peppercorns to keep the flavor tart.

To make bread crumbs, simply rub the crust and/or inside of fresh White Sage Bread (page 111) between your fingers to a fine crumb, or place day-old bread in a food processor and grind into crumbs.

WILD MINT AND LAMB SOUP

On a cold, wintry night, a steaming bowl of hearty soup can warm the chill within. This soup, with a touch of wild mint, is warming and delicious. Wild mint is customarily picked during the summer, when the herb is in season, and hung to dry in bundles in the sun. You can use either dried or fresh mint for this soup. Traditionally, this recipe is made with mutton, but I have substituted lamb because of its tenderness, taste, and availability. Either way, this is a great winter soup.

1 pound lamb stew meat, cut into 1-inch cubes
1 teaspoon salt
½ teaspoon black pepper
2 tablespoons olive oil
1 medium onion, diced
1½ cups peeled and diced carrots
1 cup diced celery
2 cloves garlic, finely chopped
3 tablespoons chopped mint leaves (fresh or dried)
4 cups water
5 cups lamb stock (page 199)
3 russet potatoes, peeled and cubed (see note)
Wild mint leaves, for garnish

Season the lamb with the salt and pepper.

In a skillet, heat 1 tablespoon olive oil over medium-high heat and add the meat. Brown for 3 minutes on each side, until the lamb is medium rare. Remove the meat from the pan and set aside.

Add the second tablespoon of olive oil to the skillet and sauté the onion, carrots, and celery over moderate heat for 2 minutes, stirring constantly. Add the garlic and sauté for 1 minute more. Remove from the heat, add the chopped mint, and set aside.

Pour the water and 4 cups of stock into a large pot and bring to a boil. Add the sautéed lamb meat, decrease the heat, and simmer for 45 minutes. Add the potatoes and simmer for another 45 minutes. Add the remaining cup of stock and the sautéed vegetables and simmer for another 15 minutes.

Garnish with wild mint leaves and serve hot with one of the traditional Indian breads. My favorite with this soup is Adobe Bread or Indian Frybread (page 68). *Serves 6*

NOTE: The cubed potatoes should be placed in a bowl of cold water until used to prevent them from turning brown. Drain the water before adding them to the soup.

Above: Grandma Susie Begay's herd of sheep in their corral.

PAN-FRIED TROUT WITH BLUE CORNMEAL, RED CHILES, AND GARLIC

6 whole river trout, 10 to 12 ounces each
1 tablespoon vegetable oil
2 cloves garlic, finely chopped, plus 6 cloves garlic,
    halved
1 egg
¼ cup milk
¾ cup blue cornmeal
1 teaspoon salt
½ teaspoon black pepper
½ cup red chile powder
4 tablespoons unsalted butter
2 dried red New Mexico or Anaheim chiles, stemmed,
    seeded, and cut into 2-inch strips

While visiting Picuris Pueblo in northern New Mexico, I asked Richard Mermejo about the fishing techniques that were used for hundreds of years before modern fishing equipment and techniques were introduced. Instead of explaining how it was done, Richard took me to a stream where he demonstrated the way his People have fished for centuries. First, he twisted together long strands of horsehair, knotted the ends, made a loop at one end, and attached the loop to the end of a long stick. He then explained how a fisherman sets the loop in a tide pool and waits for a trout to swim through the loop. When that golden opportunity arrives, the stick is jerked up to close the loop and catch the passing fish. This technique requires great skill and patience, but remarkably it is still used today, in addition to more modern techniques.

Wash each trout in cold water.

Mix together the oil and garlic and brush onto each trout.

In a medium bowl, beat together the egg and milk and set aside.

In a separate bowl, mix together the blue cornmeal, salt, pepper, and red chile powder. Dredge each trout first in the egg and milk mixture, then in the cornmeal mixture, so that each trout is thoroughly coated.

In a large skillet over moderate heat, melt the butter and add the dried red chiles and the garlic halves. Sauté for 1 minute and add the fish. Sauté the fish for 3 minutes, flip over, and sauté for another 3 minutes, until golden brown.

Serve hot on plates with the sautéed garlic and chiles. This dish goes wonderfully with Mesa Squash Fry (page 91), Posole (page 31), or sautéed red chile potatoes as a side.
Serves 6

Above: Richard Mermejo demonstrates how to use horsehair for fishing the traditional way.

PUEBLO RED CHILE STEW

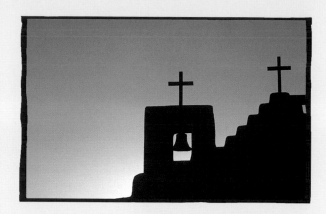

1 tablespoon olive oil
1 pound boneless chuck roast, cubed
1 onion, diced
¼ cup New Mexico or Anaheim red chile powder
(see note)
8 cups water
8 medium russet potatoes, peeled, if desired, and
cubed
1 teaspoon salt
¼ teaspoon dried oregano

Every Pueblo has a version of red chile stew that is served on their Feast Day, which is the day of the Patron Saint given to them by the Spanish. Pueblo households host visitors to their Pueblo, feeding up to several hundred people in a day. Every home table is filled with a multitude of different dishes, of which red chile stew is a favorite. Red chile stew recipes vary slightly from Pueblo to Pueblo. All are delicious and very traditional to this region. This recipe is a combination of a red chile stew that I was taught by Margaret Archuleta of Picuris Pueblo and red chile stews that I've eaten at Margie Mermejo's, also of Picuris Pueblo.

In a skillet over medium to high heat, add the oil and brown the beef for 2 minutes on each side; then decrease the heat to medium and add the onion and red chile powder, stirring constantly. Cook for 3 minutes, until the onion is translucent. Remove from the heat and set aside.

In a sauce pot, bring 6 cups of the water to a boil with the meat and dried red chile mixture. Decrease the heat and simmer, until the meat is tender, 1½ to 2 hours. Add the potatoes, salt, oregano, and the remaining 2 cups of water and continue to simmer for another 15 minutes, until the potatoes are soft.

If the stew seems too thick, add a little more water. If it is too thin, simmer a little longer until it reduces and the stew is thicker.

Serve hot. Any of the traditional Indian breads go wonderfully with this meal.
Serves 6 to 8

NOTE: Freshly ground red chile powder tends to be quite hot, but the flavor becomes less potent with time. I advise you to taste the chile powder before using it in this recipe. The amount used can be adjusted to suit your palate. Most Native cooks prepare this stew hot and pungent.

Above: San Geronimo Church, Taos Pueblo.

173

MARINATED GRILLED QUAIL

Wild game birds have been a part of the Southwest Indian diet for centuries. Quail motifs can be found on pottery in both ancient and contemporary works. Farm-raised quail is available year-round and is relatively easy to obtain (see Source Guide, page 201). This contemporary recipe for quail is served glazed on a bed of sautéed greens. An individual quail can be served as an appetizer, or two quails as a main course.

6 quail, backbones removed

MARINADE
1 tablespoon chopped fresh sage
1 tablespoon chopped fresh parsley
1 tablespoon chopped fresh rosemary
1 teaspoon salt
1 teaspoon black pepper
2 teaspoons chipotle chile powder
1 fresh serrano chile, seeded and finely chopped
½ cup olive oil
2 cloves garlic, minced
1 tablespoon lemon zest

GLAZE
4 dried red New Mexico or Anaheim chiles, stemmed
   and seeded
½ cup water
½ cup honey

GREENS
1 tablespoon olive oil
2 cloves garlic, finely chopped
2 bunches mustard greens, washed and stemmed

Wash each quail under cold running water. Cut the wings of each quail at their joints and set aside.

To make the marinade, in a mixing bowl, combine together all of the ingredients. Add the quail, making sure each quail is thoroughly coated. Cover, place in the refrigerator, and let marinate overnight.

To make the glaze, in a small saucepan, heat together the dried red chiles and water over high heat. Bring to a boil and boil for 1 minute, then remove from the heat. Let stand for 10 minutes, place the mixture into a blender, add the honey, and blend for 1 minute. Pour through a fine sieve to remove the chile skins and then discard them. Set aside.

Heat a grill or cast-iron grill pan over medium-high heat until hot but not smoking, then place the marinated quail on it. Grill for about 5 minutes, turn over and grill for another 5 minutes, then remove from the heat.

Reserve half of the glaze for serving. Brush the remaining glaze onto both sides of each grilled quail. Place the quail top-side up in a shallow roasting pan and then place them in the oven, on broil. Broil for 3 to 4 minutes until they begin to brown, then remove from the oven.

To make the greens, heat a skillet over high heat. Add the oil, then the garlic, and stir for about 15 seconds. Add the mustard greens and cook for 2 minutes, stirring constantly until the greens are tender.

Serve each quail on a bed of sautéed greens with the reserved glaze.

Serves 6 as an appetizer

NAVAJO LAMB MEAT LOAF

Meat loaf to me is comfort food. It's usually rich, simple to make, and warming to eat. This recipe was taught to me made with ground mutton or sheep, which is easy to get on many parts of the Diné (Navajo) reservation but not in many other places. Here, it is presented with ground lamb, which everyone should be able to get at their local butcher or supermarket. I especially like this dish in the winter with Indian Frybread (page 68) and homemade mashed potatoes.

1½ pounds ground lamb
2 cups peeled, seeded, and diced tomatoes
1 medium onion, finely chopped
2 cups fresh Adobe Bread Crumbs (page 68)
2 cloves garlic, finely chopped
1 teaspoon salt
½ teaspoon white pepper
½ teaspoon crushed juniper berries (see note,
    page 189)
1 egg, beaten
½ teaspoon finely chopped fresh sage leaves
1 bunch sage leaves, for garnish

Preheat the oven to 350°.

In a large bowl, combine the lamb, tomatoes, onion, bread crumbs, and garlic. Add the salt, pepper, juniper berries, egg, and sage and mix together using your hands. Be careful not to overmix; the less you mix, the lighter and fluffier the meat loaf will be when cooked.

Place the mixture in a loaf pan and bake for 45 minutes to 1 hour. Garnish with the sage leaves and serve hot.
Serves 6 to 8

TROUT WRAPPED IN BACON AND BAKED IN CLAY

In this recipe, New Mexican clay is molded around fresh trout that has been stuffed with fresh herbs, wrapped in bacon, and then baked in an oven. Walter Whitewater, a traditional Navajo and contemporary chef, remembers stories he was told of food being baked in clay in open fires until the clay split open and the food was eaten. The clay keeps the trout moist and seals in the flavor of the herbs and bacon. It is one of the best baked fish dishes I have ever eaten.

12 to 15 dried corn husks

9 pounds non-toxic terra-cotta clay (1½ pounds per trout) (see note)

12 large sprigs thyme

12 whole fresh sage leaves

6 whole fresh trout, 10 to 12 ounces each

1½ teaspoons salt

1½ teaspoons black pepper

6 pieces thick bacon

Soak the corn husks in warm water for about 10 minutes until pliable. Remove from the water and set aside.

Divide the clay into six equal portions. Take one portion of the clay and, with a rolling pin, roll out the clay like a dough to about ¼ inch thick. Make sure it is the length of the trout plus 1 inch to ensure that the trout will fit into the clay covering.

Stuff 2 sprigs of thyme and 2 sage leaves inside of each trout. Sprinkle the salt and pepper inside and outside of each trout. Cut each piece of bacon in half and wrap one piece around the base of each trout and another around the top of the trout.

Place the corn husks with the narrow side out, or lengthwise, and completely wrap them around each trout. Overlap the corn husks so that no part of the trout is exposed. You will need about 2 or 3 corn husks per trout, depending on their size. (The purpose of the corn husks is to cover the trout completely so that the fish does not stick to the clay.)

Cut each piece of clay in half lengthwise with a knife. Place a wrapped trout on top of one of the pieces of clay. Cover with a second piece of clay and seal the edges with your fingers. Make 3 small slits with a knife on the top of each clay-covered trout.

Preheat the oven to 500°. Place the clay-covered trout on a baking sheet and bake for 20 minutes. Remove from the oven and let cool. When the clay-covered trout is cool enough to handle, crack it open with a kitchen mallet or press down near the air vent slits with your hands. The clay will peel off with ease and can then be discarded. Serve the trout whole in the corn husks.

Serves 6

NOTE: Check in your area to see what types of clay are available that are non-toxic and safe to cook with. I have listed the source for the clay we used here in Santa Fe in the Source Guide (page 201).

Opposite: Miniature pottery made by Tracy Kavena (Hopi).

ELK TENDERLOIN WITH GOOSEBERRY SAUCE

This is a contemporary recipe for elk meat developed by Sam Etheridge, former executive chef at the Bien Shur restaurant at the Sandia Casino in Albuquerque. It was some of the best game meat Walter Whitewater and I had ever had; it was tender and had a delicious flavor complemented by the gooseberry sauce. Contemporary chefs often use wine for marinating game meats; the alcohol pulls out any gamey flavor and is then discarded. However, if you do not want to use alcohol, you can substitute purple grape juice for the wine in this recipe.

MARINADE

1 cup unsweetened purple grape juice or red wine
½ cup olive oil
1 tablespoon chopped fresh rosemary leaves
1 tablespoon chopped fresh thyme

2 pieces of elk tenderloin (about 2 pounds total),
    venison or beef can be substituted

GOOSEBERRY SAUCE

1 cup dried gooseberries
1 cup black cherry juice
2 cups veal stock (page 200)
1 teaspoon salt
1 teaspoon black pepper

To make the marinade, in a bowl large enough to fit the elk tenderloin, mix all of the ingredients together and spread evenly over the meat. Cover with plastic wrap and let marinate in the refrigerator for 24 hours.

To make the sauce, in a saucepan, combine the gooseberries and cherry juice. Heat over medium heat until the mixture has reduced and is syrupy, about 10 minutes. Add the stock, salt, and pepper and simmer for another 15 minutes. Remove from the heat and set aside.

Remove the meat from the refrigerator and wipe the marinade from the meat with a pastry brush or with your hands. This will remove the gamey flavor that was released into the marinade. Discard the marinade.

Heat a grill or cast-iron grill pan over medium-high heat until very hot but not quite smoking. If you cook the elk on a cast-iron grill pan indoors make sure to turn on your stove fan as the room will get smoky while the meat cooks. Cook the tenderloins for about 5 minutes on each side for medium-rare meat and longer for more well done.

Slice the elk tenderloin at an angle into slices about ½ inch thick. Reheat the gooseberry sauce and spoon on top of the elk. Serve immediately.
Serves 6

NOTE: On many reservations today alcohol is prohibited, and so it is not customary to use wine in cooking. Wine reductions, however, add a marvelous flavor to sauces, and many contemporary chefs are using them today when cooking game meat. If you wish you can substitute red wine for the unsweetened grape juice.

ROAST DOVE WITH BLACK WALNUT, WHITE SAGE, AND ADOBE BREAD STUFFING

The dove is one of the few wild game birds in the Southwest seen throughout the mesas, the high desert regions, and in the southern deserts. It makes a wonderful meal, especially when complemented by black walnuts (Juglans major), which are found growing along streams and in canyons in upper deserts of Arizona, and white sage (Artemisia tridentata), which grows wild throughout parts of Arizona and in northern New Mexico.

BLACK WALNUT, WHITE SAGE, AND ADOBE BREAD STUFFING

½ teaspoon crushed juniper berries (see note, page 189)

1 cup water

¾ cup chopped black walnuts

2 cups Adobe Bread Crumbs (page 68)

½ cup chopped fresh chives

½ teaspoon salt

½ teaspoon black pepper

2 tablespoons dried white sage

ROAST DOVE

6 doves or squab, or 3 Cornish game hens

2 tablespoons plus 2 teaspoons dried white sage

6 whole fresh chives

1 tablespoon unsalted butter, melted

½ teaspoon salt

½ teaspoon white pepper

To make the stuffing, in a small saucepan, bring the juniper berries and water to a boil over high heat and cook for about 5 minutes to reduce the liquid by half. Strain the liquid through a fine sieve to remove the berries.

Combine the walnuts, bread crumbs, chives, salt, black pepper, sage, and the juniper-berry water in a bowl. Stir together with a large spoon.

To prepare the doves, remove and discard the giblets from each bird, rinse thoroughly, and pat dry.

Preheat the oven to 450°.

Sprinkle 1 teaspoon of the sage underneath the skins of each of the birds, then fill each bird's cavity with some of the stuffing. Tuck the wings under and tie the legs together with the whole chives. Brush each bird with butter and sprinkle with the salt, white pepper, and the remaining 2 teaspoons sage.

Bake the birds in a shallow baking dish for 40 minutes for doves and squabs, or 1 hour for game hens, until they are golden brown and thoroughly cooked.

Serves 6

NOTE: Doves may be hard to obtain commercially, as they are a wild game bird. Squab or Cornish game hens will work wonderfully with this recipe.

Above: Juanita (Tita) Garcia (Hopi) harvesting wild edible herbs.

HOW TO DRESS A RABBIT

If you buy a rabbit from a butcher, he will prepare the legs and tenderloins for you. Remember to also ask for the carcass, which can be used for stock. If you buy whole rabbits, you will have to dress them yourself.

With a sharp boning knife, cut the hind legs from the body of a whole rabbit. Place a leg flat on a cutting board and run the tip of the knife along the thigh bone, removing the bone from joint to joint. Repeat the same process with the other hind leg and set aside.

Place the carcass skin-side up and breast down. With a knife, cut along the backbone, releasing the meat from the spine of the lower shoulder to the upper rump. Run the knife along the ribs and down the side of the rabbit to release the tenderloin.

Place the tenderloin flat on the cutting surface and remove the silver skin and any excess fat.

The tenderloin and legs can be used for cooked rabbit recipes and the carcass for stock.

RABBIT WITH BLUE CORNMEAL AND WILD MINT SAUCE

For years, rabbits were hunted frequently by many tribes in the Southwest and provided a major source of meat. Although venison was prized, rabbits supplied a large portion of meat, not only for sustenance, but also to fulfill many ceremonial obligations, including prayers and offerings. In most states, domestic rabbit is available through specialty meat markets and breeders. Usually you can just purchase the legs and tenderloins, but I like to buy the whole rabbit so I can make stock with the remaining parts and bones of the carcass.

RABBIT WITH BLUE CORNMEAL

Tenderloins and legs of 3 (2-pound) rabbits (opposite page)
1 teaspoon salt
1 teaspoon white pepper
1 cup Blue Cornbread crumbs (see note)
8 tablespoons finely chopped fresh mint leaves
4 tablespoons safflower oil
3 tablespoons Dijon or other spicy mustard

WILD MINT SAUCE

3 cups rabbit stock (page 199)
2 tablespoons unsalted butter, softened
½ cup finely chopped fresh mint leaves

Preheat the oven to 500°.

Season the rabbit with the salt and pepper. Mix together the bread crumbs and mint and set aside.

Pour the oil into an ovenproof sauté pan and sear the legs on each side over high heat until golden brown, about 4 minutes. Add the tenderloins and sear them on both sides until golden brown, about 1½ minutes.

Remove the rabbit from the sauté pan and drain the oil. Return the rabbit to the pan and place in the oven for 10 to 15 minutes, until the tenderloins and legs are firm to the touch. Puncture the flesh with a sharp knife; if the juices run clear, the rabbit is fully cooked.

While the rabbit is cooking, prepare the mint sauce. Put the stock in a saucepan and reduce it by half over moderate heat, about 15 minutes. Add the butter and mint and bring to a boil. Decrease the heat and keep the sauce warm until the rabbit is cooked.

Remove the sauté pan from the oven and let cool for a few minutes. With a basting brush, evenly brush the mustard onto the surface of the legs and tenderloins. Then lightly press a ¼-inch-thick coating of the bread crumb–mint mixture onto the legs and tenderloins.

Turn the oven to broil. Place the rabbit back in the oven until the bread crumbs start to brown and the rabbit is piping hot, about 2 minutes. Serve immediately with the mint sauce.
Serves 6

NOTES: It is important to know that rabbits do carry disease, as do other types of wild game, and should only be killed and skinned by experienced hunters.

To make bread crumbs, simply rub the crust and/ or inside of fresh Blue Cornbread (page 52) between your fingers to a fine crumb, or place day-old bread in a food processor and grind into crumbs.

SUMMER VEGETABLE AND CATFISH CASSEROLE

This casserole bakes together fall harvest vegetables and catfish fillets. We baked this dish in black clay earthenware that can be used on the stovetop or in the oven. Clay earthenware seals in the delicious flavor of the vegetables as well as the fish fillets, making for a hearty meal.

2 yellow squash, cut into ¼-inch slices
2 zucchini, cut into ¼-inch slices
4 plum tomatoes, cut into ¼-inch slices lengthwise
1 tablespoon olive oil
Juice of 2 fresh lemons
1 clove garlic, finely chopped
1 teaspoon New Mexico or Anaheim red chile
   powder
1 teaspoon salt
½ teaspoon black pepper
1 medium red bell pepper
1 cup corn kernels (fresh, frozen, or canned)
1 leek, white and green parts, diced
¼ cup heavy cream
½ cup fish stock (page 198)
4 catfish fillets (about ½ pound each)
1 tablespoon fresh thyme, finely chopped
1½ tablespoons butter

In a bowl, combine the yellow squash, zucchini, and tomato slices. Add the olive oil, lemon juice, garlic, red chile powder, and half of the salt and black pepper. Mix together to thoroughly coat the vegetables and set aside.

Roast the red bell pepper using the open flame method (page 61), then peel, seed, and dice it.

Cut the fresh corn kernels from the cob. In a small saucepan, blanch them in boiling water until cooked, 3 to 4 minutes.

In a separate bowl, combine the leek, corn kernels, and diced red bell pepper. Mix together and set aside.

In a 10 by 12 by 2-inch casserole dish, make a single layer of the yellow squash, zucchini, and tomato slice mixture, until you have covered the bottom. Make a second layer with one-half of the leek, corn, and roasted red pepper mixture.

Repeat the process until you have 3 layers of the yellow squash, zucchini, and tomato mixture, and 2 layers of the leek, corn, and roasted red pepper mixture.

Preheat the oven to 350°.

Pour the heavy cream and fish stock on top of the layered vegetables in the casserole dish and bake for 15 minutes. Remove from the heat and place the catfish fillets on top. Sprinkle with the chopped thyme and the remaining salt and black pepper. Place ¼ table spoon of butter on each of the catfish fillets and return the casserole dish to the oven. Bake uncovered for an additional 10 minutes, until the catfish fillets are cooked. Serve immediately.
Serves 6

VENISON STEAK WITH JUNIPER BERRY AND FIERY RED CHILE SAUCE

In the high-altitude areas of the Southwest, deer meat, or venison, is widely eaten by Native Americans. Until recently, wild venison could only be obtained by cooks with a hunter in the family. Now, it can be obtained in specialty meat stores and by mail order (see Source Guide, page 201). This recipe is prepared over an open grill, which enhances the delicious flavor of the venison; however, it can also be prepared in your kitchen.

JUNIPER BERRY AND FIERY RED CHILE SAUCE

2 tablespoons dried juniper berries (see note)

3 cups unsweetened dark grape juice (see note)

2 bay leaves

1½ teaspoons dried thyme

2 shallots, peeled and coarsely chopped

2 cups veal stock (page 200)

4 whole dried chiles de árbol

VENISON STEAKS

6 venison steaks, 8 to 10 ounces each

2 tablespoons olive oil

1 tablespoon salt

1 tablespoon black pepper

To make the sauce, wrap the juniper berries in a clean kitchen towel and crush them using a mallet or heavy skillet. Remove them from the towel and place in a saucepan with the grape juice, bay leaves, thyme, and shallots. Simmer over medium heat for 20 to 25 minutes, until the liquid has reduced to 1 cup.

Add the veal stock, bring to a boil, then decrease the heat to medium and simmer for another 15 minutes, until the sauce has reduced to 1½ cups.

While the sauce is reducing, place the chiles in a small bowl and remove their stems and seeds. With your fingers, tear the chiles into pieces about the size of small beans. (If you are sensitive to chiles, wear gloves to tear the chiles into pieces.) Set aside.

Remove the sauce from the heat and pass it through a fine sieve to remove the herb leaves and berry skins.

Heat the coals in an open grill until very hot (or heat a grill pan over high heat until very hot).

Brush each of the steaks on both sides with the olive oil and season with the salt and pepper.

Place the steaks on the grill and cook for about 3 minutes, until they have charred marks. Rotate the steaks a half turn and grill for another 3 minutes, until the steaks have a cross-hatched charred pattern.

Flip the steaks over and grill about 5 minutes more, until done as desired.

Ladle the sauce onto each plate, top with the steaks, patterned-side up, and sprinkle with the chile peppers. *Serves 6*

NOTES: Juniper berries gathered on the reservation from the one-seeded juniper (*Juniperus monosperma*) have a light and delicate flavor; commercially sold berries tend to be more aromatic and pungent. If you use store-bought juniper berries, use half the amount.

On many reservations today alcohol is prohibited, and so it is not customary to use wine in cooking. Wine reductions, however, add a marvelous flavor to sauces, and many contemporary chefs are using them today when cooking game meat. If you wish, you can substitute red wine for the unsweetened grape juice.

CORIANDER-CURED RACK OF VENISON
WITH DRIED CHERRY SAUCE

Unless you have a hunter in your family, rack of venison may not be one of the dishes you would normally prepare. Sam Etheridge, former executive chef at Bien Shur restaurant at the Sandia Pueblo casino in Albuquerque, who is excellent with cooking game meats, shared this contemporary recipe for venison chops with me. It can be made with either wild or farm-raised venison. Farm-raised venison is now more readily available (see Source Guide, page 201) and makes a delicious winter meal. The venison is cured overnight, then baked in the oven and served with a dried cherry sauce, resulting in meat that is tender and delicious without a strong gamey flavor.

1 rack of venison (about 2 pounds)
1 tablespoon olive oil

CORIANDER RUB

2 teaspoons whole coriander
1 teaspoon whole cumin seed
1 teaspoon whole fennel seed
1 teaspoon whole black peppercorns
1 teaspoon dried thyme
1 teaspoon New Mexico or Anaheim red chile
   powder
1 teaspoon salt

DRIED CHERRY SAUCE

¾ cup dried black cherries
3 cups black cherry juice
2 cups veal stock (page 200)

Trim any fat from the venison rack chops and remove any meat from the rib bones. Set aside.

Preheat the oven to 350°.

To make the coriander rub, combine all the ingredients together. Place the mixture in a small baking pan and toast the spices in the oven for 5 minutes. Remove from the oven and let cool. Grind together in a spice grinder. Remove from the grinder and rub the spice mixture onto both sides of the rack of venison to cover all of the meat. Place the venison rack in a baking pan, cover, and let sit overnight in the refrigerator.

To make the sauce, combine the black cherries with the black cherry juice in a saucepan. Cook over medium heat for 15 minutes, stirring occasionally, until it reduces into a syrup. Add the veal stock, bring to a boil, then decrease the heat and simmer for 20 minutes. Cover and refrigerate.

The next day, remove the venison rack from the refrigerator. Preheat the oven to 400°. In a skillet over high heat, heat the olive oil until hot but not smoking. Sear the venison rack for 3 minutes on both sides, then remove from the heat. Place the venison rack in a roasting pan and bake for 15 minutes for medium-rare, longer for more well-done meat. Remove from the oven and let rest for 5 minutes. Slice the chops from the rack and serve hot with some of the reheated cherry sauce spooned on top. Serve immediately.
Serves 6

Above: Petroglyph from Galisteo Basin in New Mexico.

STUFFED DOVE WITH SAUTÉED PURSLANE

Purslane (Portulaca oleracea), known to the Hopi as peehala, and also called verdolagas throughout New Mexico, is a small plant with succulent, fleshy leaves that grows in sandy soil during the warm, moist summer months in the Southwest. Like a cactus, the leaves of purslane retain water and become juicier the more it rains. Although the entire plant may be eaten, the smaller stems and younger leaves have a sweeter, more delicate taste than the larger stems. Purslane has a variety of uses and can be used much like watercress, which is a fine substitution if purslane is hard to obtain in your area.

STUFFED DOVE

6 doves or squab, or 3 Cornish game hens

5 dried red New Mexico or Anaheim chiles, stemmed and seeded

2 cups Adobe Bread Crumbs (page 68)

2 cups (¼ pound) purslane or watercress, cleaned, stemmed, and chopped

3 cloves garlic, finely chopped

1 teaspoon salt

½ teaspoon white pepper

¼ cup chicken stock (page 198)

1 tablespoon unsalted butter, melted

SAUTÉED PURSLANE

2 tablespoons unsalted butter

3 cloves garlic, halved

9 cups (about 1 pound) purslane or watercress, cleaned, stemmed, and chopped

1 teaspoon salt

½ teaspoon white pepper

Dried red chiles, coarsely chopped, for garnish

Preheat the oven to 400°.

Remove and discard the giblets from each bird, rinse thoroughly, and pat dry.

Soak the dried red chiles in 4 cups of warm water for 5 minutes, until they are soft. Drain and dice the chiles.

For the stuffing, combine the bread crumbs, chopped greens, chiles, garlic, salt, pepper, and chicken stock and mix together in a bowl.

Fill each bird's cavity with stuffing. Tie the legs together with a string or strand of a dried corn husk. Rub the skin of each bird with the melted butter.

Cook in a large roasting pan, 40 minutes for doves or squabs or 1 hour for game hens, until the birds are tender, juicy, golden brown, and thoroughly cooked.

To make the sautéed purslane, in a large skillet, melt the butter over medium-high heat. Add the garlic and sauté for 2 minutes, until lightly browned. Stir constantly to avoid burning or sticking.

Add the greens and stir so they are evenly coated with the butter. Sprinkle with the salt and pepper and cook for 2 to 4 minutes, until they are soft.

Arrange some of the greens on each plate and put one roast dove or squab or half a game hen on top. Garnish with the dried red chiles.

Serves 6

RED CHILE PIÑON-CRUSTED LAMB CHOPS

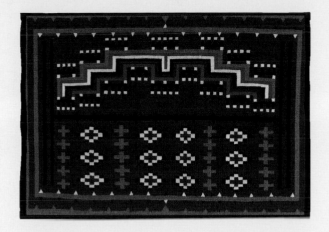

Walter Whitewater, a traditional Diné (Navajo) and contemporary chef, grew up around a sheepherding tradition. His grandmother, Susie Begay, and his aunts have always herded sheep for their meat and their wool and continue to do so today. Walter has eaten sheep prepared every way imaginable, and he continues to experiment with new ways to prepare sheep and lamb. Together with Sam Etheridge, the former executive chef at Bien Shur restaurant at the Sandia Pueblo casino, Walter developed this recipe for lamb using a rub made from piñons. Two racks of lamb are cooked with this delicious crust; then, the meat is cut from the rack and served with red chile sauce (made from chile powder).

2 full racks of lamb (16 to 18 chops) (see Source
    Guide, page 201)
2¼ cups Red Chile Sauce #2 (page 64)
1 tablespoon olive oil
1 cup Adobe Bread Crumbs (page 68)
1 cup piñons (pine nuts)
1 tablespoon unsalted butter, softened
1 teaspoon salt
½ teaspoon black pepper

Cut the fat off the back end of the bones of the lamb racks and trim any fat off the chops (or you can ask your butcher to do this for you). Rub ¾ cup of the red chile sauce on both sides of each lamb rack, place in a bowl, cover, and let marinate in the refrigerator overnight.

The next day, remove the lamb from the refrigerator and brush off any excess marinade and discard. Preheat the oven to 400°. In a skillet over medium-high heat, add the oil and sear the lamb racks for about 2 minutes on each side, until brown. Remove the meat from the skillet and set aside.

In a food processor, pulse the Adobe Bread Crumbs until finely ground into small crumbs. Add the piñons and pulse again for 30 seconds, until the nuts are coarsely ground. Add the butter, salt, and pepper and pulse for an additional 15 seconds. You will have a dough that is moist and sticks together when pressed with your fingers. Remove the dough from the food processor and place into a bowl.

With your fingers, press the dough onto the back sides of the rib racks, covering each lamb chop all the way up to the exposed bone, until the meat on the lamb racks are completely covered. The crust should be about ¼ inch thick.

Place the crusted lamb racks with the crust-sides up in a roasting pan and bake for 12 minutes for medium rare chops or longer for more well-done chops. Remove from the oven and place the racks on a wood cutting board.

Place the remaining chile sauce in a saucepan and heat over medium heat until warm. Slice the chops from the racks and serve 2 to 3 chops per person with about ¼ cup of the chile sauce. These lamb chops can be served with homemade mashed potatoes, Mesa Squash Fry (page 91), Sautéed Purslane (page 193), and Indian Frybread (page 68) or freshly baked White Sage Bread (page 111). *Serves 6*

Above: Diné (Navajo) rug from Forest Lake, Arizona, and woven by the Jim family.

MEAT JERKY

Annabel Eagle, an elder woman of the Southern Ute tribe in Colorado, recounted to me the traditional process of preparing meat jerky. Her husband hunted game—traditionally, elk, venison, and rabbit—and Annabel's challenge was to cut the longest and thinnest strips of meat possible, because these dry more quickly and are less likely to spoil. After generously salting the meat, Annabel would put the strips on drying racks in the hot sun for 3 to 4 days, taking them inside at night to keep the meat away from prowling animals. Today, an easier, less time-consuming technique has been adopted by many of the younger generation. I have used beef for this recipe rather than game meats because beef is easier to obtain. However, if you have a hunter in the family or access to game meat, this recipe will work for game meats as well.

1 pound tip roast, flank steak, or other lean cut of beef, cut ¼ inch thick
1½ teaspoons kosher salt
1½ teaspoons chopped dried chile pequín
1½ tablespoons olive oil

Cut the beef into strips about 2 inches wide and 8 to 10 inches long.

Mix the salt, chile pequín, and oil together and rub into both sides of the meat strips with your fingers. Marinate in the refrigerator for 6 to 8 hours.

If using an electric oven, preheat the oven to 200°. If using a gas oven, the warmth of the pilot light will be sufficient to dry the jerky. Place the meat strips on a wire rack over a pan to catch the drippings and slowly cook in the oven with the door ajar for 9 hours, then turn the strips over and cook for another 9 hours. The jerky should be medium-dry but not completely dehydrated. If it is not medium-dry, cook it a little longer.
Makes about 15 strips of jerky

VARIATION: Different spices can be added to the jerky along with the oil, salt, and chile. Add ½ teaspoon dried oregano for oregano jerky, ½ teaspoon dried cumin for cumin jerky, or 2 finely chopped cloves garlic for garlic jerky.

Opposite: Cows grazing on the Diné (Navajo) Reservation near Dilkon, Arizona (top). Paul C. Begaye Tohlaki, Diné (Navajo) from Pinon, Arizona, riding his horse Tobey (bottom).

STOCKS

FISH STOCK

Jeff Koscomb at Above Sea Level, a wholesale fish supplier in Santa Fe, New Mexico, was kind enough to supply us with fish bones for all of our stocks. Check in your area to see if there is a supplier or grocer that will sell you fish bones for your own fish stock.

4 to 6 pounds halibut or other white fish bones, with the heads and tails on
3 carrots, coarsely chopped
2 celery stalks, coarsely chopped
2 large onions, quartered
2 bay leaves
1 bunch fresh parsley, coarsely chopped
1 tablespoon black peppercorns
5 quarts water

Rinse the fish bones under cold running water and remove the gills.

In a large stockpot, combine the fish bones, carrots, celery, onions, bay leaves, parsley, peppercorns, and water and bring to a boil over high heat. Decrease the heat and simmer for 45 minutes, until the stock has reduced by half. Skim the top frequently to remove the foam.

Remove from the heat and pour through a fine sieve lined with cheesecloth. Discard the contents of the sieve. Pour into a container and place in the refrigerator. The stock will keep for 5 days in a covered container. *Makes about 2½ quarts*

NOTE: Although better fresh, stock can also be frozen in ice cube trays; the cubes can be stored in plastic bags in the freezer for several months. Larger quantities of stock can be poured into sealed containers or directly into plastic freezer bags and stored in the freezer.

CHICKEN STOCK

I have found that it is easiest to prepare stock by cooking two chickens, making a meal out of the roasted chicken, and then using the leftover bones for making this stock. You can also buy whole uncooked chickens and fillet them yourself, retaining the bones for your stock. Either way, I would still recommend roasting the bones, as it gives the stock a better flavor.

2 large chicken carcasses or whole chickens
Salt
Pepper
2 tablespoons fresh or dried rosemary leaves
4 celery stalks, coarsely chopped
4 large carrots, coarsely chopped
2 large leeks, white and green parts, coarsely chopped
2 medium yellow onions, quartered
1 bunch fresh parsley, coarsely chopped
3 bay leaves
1 bunch fresh thyme
8 quarts water

Preheat the oven to 350°. Season the chickens with salt and pepper and cover with the rosemary leaves. Cover and roast for one hour. Remove the cover and brown the chickens in the oven until cooked, another 30 to 45 minutes. Remove all the meat from the bones and reserve for another use. If you are just roasting the bones, turn them every 20 minutes for 1 hour, then remove and set aside.

Combine the bones, celery, carrots, leeks, onions, parsley, bay leaves, thyme, and water in a stockpot and bring to a boil over medium-high heat. Decrease the heat to low and simmer for about 1 hour, skimming off the fat as it rises to the surface. Continue simmering over low heat until the stock has been reduced by one-third.

Remove from the heat and carefully strain the stock through a sieve lined with cheesecloth. Discard the contents of the sieve. Pour the stock into a container and let cool. Then place the stock in the refrigerator for 3 hours. Remove any solidified fat from the top. The stock will keep for 5 days in a covered container in the refrigerator. *Makes about 5 quarts*

LAMB STOCK

Most restaurants and professional chefs use stocks to make reductions and sauces. The flavor of meat stocks comes from the bones and it is a delicious and healthy way to make sauces and soup bases for stews, which can be frozen for later use. Many Native American households will prepare soups and stews with the bones and then remove them before serving, which is basically the same as making a stock. This stock is delicious and is a good way to make use of the bones from the butchered meat of a lamb or sheep.

5 pounds lamb shank bones or lamb loin bones
1 tablespoon olive oil
5 ripe tomatoes, quartered
2 leeks, white and green parts, coarsely chopped
5 celery stalks, coarsely chopped
4 large carrots, coarsely chopped
6 quarts water
4 bay leaves
½ bunch fresh parsley, coarsely chopped
2 bunches fresh thyme
2 bunches fresh rosemary

Preheat the oven to 450°. Put the bones in a large roasting pan and brown them for about 1 hour, turning them every 20 minutes. Remove from the oven and set aside.

In a large stock pot, heat the oil, add the tomatoes, leeks, celery, and carrots, and sauté over high heat for 15 minutes, stirring constantly.

Add the bones, water, and herbs and bring to a boil over medium heat. Decrease the heat and simmer for 4½ to 5 hours, skimming the surface every half hour.

Remove from the heat and pour the stock through a sieve lined with cheesecloth. Discard the contents of the sieve. Refrigerate the stock for 3 hours, then remove the solidified fat from the top. The stock will keep for 5 days in a covered container in the refrigerator.
Makes about 4 quarts

RABBIT STOCK

I always use whole rabbits when cooking rabbit dishes, whether they are from a hunt or bought at my butcher. Then, I dress the rabbit, reserve the meat portions I will use for my recipes, and make stock from the bones. Stocks are very nutritious and nothing is wasted as all parts of the animal are used. I suggest you do the same whenever you make rabbit dishes. The additional stock can be frozen for later use.

2 carcasses from 2-pound rabbits, cut into thirds
1 tablespoon olive oil
3 carrots, coarsely chopped
3 celery stalks, coarsely chopped
3 small onions, quartered
2 bay leaves
1 small bunch fresh thyme
1 bunch fresh parsley, coarsely chopped
5 quarts water

Preheat the oven to 500°. Place the carcasses in a roasting pan and bake for 40 minutes, turning occasionally, until they are crisp and browned.

To a large stockpot, add the oil, carrots, celery, onions, bay leaves, thyme, and parsley, and sauté over moderately high heat for 3 minutes. Add the water and carcasses and bring to a boil over high heat, then decrease the heat and simmer for 3 hours, until the stock has reduced by half. Skim the top of the stock occasionally to remove the foam. Remove from the heat and pour through a sieve. Discard the contents of the sieve.

Set aside to cool. Refrigerate for several hours, then remove the solidified fat from the top. The stock will keep for 5 days in a covered container in the refrigerator.
Makes about 2½ quarts

VEAL STOCK

The flavor of veal stock is unlike that of any other stock; it has a distinctively delicious taste. I strongly advise you to use veal stock when it is suggested in a recipe. The loin bone and knuckles can be purchased from your local butcher. Be sure to ask for bones with the marrow, which contains most of the flavor. I usually make large quantities of stocks and freeze portions for later use.

5 pounds veal or beef bones (loin, knuckle, or both)
1 tablespoon olive oil
5 ripe tomatoes, quartered
2 leeks, white and green parts, coarsely chopped
5 celery stalks, coarsely chopped
4 large carrots, coarsely chopped
6 quarts water
4 bay leaves
1 bunch fresh parsley, coarsely chopped
2 bunches fresh thyme

Preheat the oven to 450°. Put the bones in a large roasting pan and brown them for about 1 hour, turning them every 20 minutes. Remove them from the oven and set aside.

In a large stock pot, combine the oil, tomatoes, leeks, celery, and carrots and sauté over high heat for 15 minutes, stirring constantly.

Add the bones, water, and herbs and bring to a boil over medium heat. Decrease the heat and simmer for 4½ to 5 hours, skimming the surface every half hour until all the remnants of fat and foam disappear. Some cooks let the stock simmer overnight for a darker stock. Remove from the heat and carefully strain the stock through a sieve lined with cheesecloth. Discard the contents of the sieve.

Refrigerate the stock for 3 hours, then remove the solidified fat from the top. The stock will keep for 5 days covered in the refrigerator. Once refrigerated, it will turn into a gelatin, similar to aspic, which is normal. It will turn back to liquid once it is reheated.

Makes about 4 quarts

CREDITS

SOUTHWESTERN NATIVE AMERICAN ARTIFACTS
Special thanks to Philip Garaway of the Native American Art Gallery in Venice, California, for supplying the artifacts that appear in the following photographs:

Pages 22–23, 31, and 40: Salado stone matate and grinding stone, central Arizona, circa 1300.

Pages 24, 38, and 144: Navajo (Diné) wedding basket, circa 1970s.

Pages 28 and 88: Hopi *piki* tray, circa 1970s.

Page 40: Roosevelt black-on-white pottery olla, Mogollon Culture, central Arizona, circa 1250–1300.

Page 123: Coiled Apache basket-tray, central Arizona, circa 1910–1920.

Page 154: Santa Clara black plainware bowl, northern New Mexico, circa 1920s; Jeddito black-on-yellow ladles, Hopi, northeastern Arizona, circa 1325–1600.

Page 156: Coiled Apache pictorial baskets, Arizona, circa 1910–1920.

Page 189: Hopi coil basket, Second Mesa, Arizona, circa 1980s.

OTHER MATERIALS
Special thanks to the Kavenas for lending their contemporary pottery, and to Cookworks, Inc. for providing many of the contemporary plates in the food photos of this cookbook.

Kavena Pottery, Juanita and Tracy Kavena, *Hopi* Polacca, Arizona, circa 1980s, pages 112 and 178.

Traditional mica pottery, Tesuque Pueblo, circa 1980s, page 36.

Navajo (Diné) rug woven by Susie Begay, circa 1980s, pages 142–43.

Cookworks, Inc., Plates & Flatware, pages 42, 48, 86, 94, 140, 153, 166, 168, 190, and 194.
316 Guadalupe Street
Santa Fe, NM 87501
(505) 988-7676

American Home Furnishings Plates, pages 46, 93, 130, 174, and 180.

SOURCE GUIDE

BUENO FOODS
P.O. Box 293
Albuquerque, NM 87103
1-800-95-CHILE
(505) 243-2722
Chiles, blue corn, dry posole

CASADOS FARMS
P.O. Box 1269
San Juan Pueblo, NM 87566
(505) 852-2433
Hominy, posole, *blue corn flour, other corn products, chiles, chile powders,* chicos, *and beans*

CHERI'S DESERT HARVEST
1840 E. Winsett
Tucson, AZ 85719
(520) 623-4141
Prickly pear products, chiles

CERAMIC KING
3300 Girard NE
Albuquerque, NM 87107
1-800-781-2529
(505) 881-2350
New Mexico clay (for baking)

COOKWORKS, INC.
316 Guadalupe Street
Santa Fe, NM 87501
(505) 988-7676
Yellow and blue cornmeal, anasazi beans, chile powders, posole, *and spices*

GENEVIEVE KAURSGOWVA
P.O. Box 772
Hotevilla, AZ 86030
Piki *bread and culinary ash*

LOS CHILEROS
P.O. Box 6215
Santa Fe, NM 87501
(505) 471-6967
www.loschileros.com
Blue corn products, dried chiles, piñons, herbs, spices, hominy, and posole

MOUNTAINAIR MEATS
Seva Dubuar
2910A San Isidro Ct.
Santa Fe, NM 87507
(505) 438-4965
Toll Free 1-866-466-6328
All types of wild game birds, game meats, and lamb

NATIVE SEEDS/SEARCH
526 N. 4th Avenue
Tucson, AZ 85705-8450
(520) 622-5561
www.nativeseeds.org
e-mail: info@nativeseeds.org
A non-profit organization supplying all types of heirloom seeds, including chiles, corn, squash, beans, melons. Corn flours, wide range of corn products, whole dried chiles, chile powders, beans, nopalitos, mesquite flour, herbs, teas, prickly pear sweets, and more. Call for catalog.

NIMAN RANCH
1025 E. 12th Street
Oakland, CA 94606
(510) 808-0330
www.nimanranch.com
Natural lamb and lamb products

NORTHERN NEW MEXICO PRODUCTS
M & S Farms
P.O. Box 220
Alcalde, NM 87511
(505) 852-4368
Posole, *hominy,* chicos, *ground corn flour, other corn products, dried chiles, and chile powders*

SAN JUAN AGRICULTURAL COOPERATIVE
P.O. Box 1188
San Juan Pueblo, NM 87566
(505) 836-0825
www.puebloharvest.com
Dried corn, dried whole green chiles, dried fruit, and chicos

SANTA FE SCHOOL OF COOKING
116 W. San Francisco Street
Santa Fe, NM 87501
(505) 983-4511
www.santafeschoolofcooking.com
All types of chiles and chile powders, posole, chicos, *corn products,* huitlacoche, azafrán, *herbs, prickly pear syrup, black pottery, cookware, and spices*

TEXAS WILD GAME COOPERATIVE
Broken Arrow Ranch
P.O. Box 530
Ingram, TX 78025
1-800-962-GAME
www.brokenarrow.com
Free-range venison, antelope

VALLEY DISTRIBUTING COMPANY, INC.
2819 Second Street, N.W.
Albuquerque, NM 87107
(505) 344-1623
Piñons

ZENITRAM INDUSTRIES
P.O. Box 52
El Rito, NM 87530
(505) 581-4576
Natural lamb and lamb prodcuts

BIBLIOGRAPHY

Andrews, Jean. 1984. *Peppers: The Domesticated Capsicums.* Austin: University of Texas Press.

Berry, Elizabeth, and Florence Fabricant. 1999. *The Great Bean Book.* Berkeley, Calif.: Ten Speed Press.

Buskirk, Winfred. 1949. *Western Apache Subsistence Economy.* Unpublished Ph.D. dissertation for the University of New Mexico.

_____. 1986. *The Western Apache.* Norman: University of Oklahoma Press. Bye, Robert A., Jr., and Rita A. Shuster.

Carson, Dale. 1996. *New Native American Cooking.* New York: Random House.

Castetter, Edward, and Ruth Underhill. 1935. "Ethnobiological Studies in the American Southwest II: Ethnobiology of the Papago Indians." *New Mexico Bulletin,* vol. 4, no. 3, Biological Series.

Castetter, Edward, and Willis H. Bell. 1951. *Yuman Indian Agriculture.* Albuquerque: University of New Mexico Press.

Champagne, Duane. 1994. *Native America; Portrait of the Peoples.* Detroit, MI.: Visible Ink.

Cordell, Linda S. 1994. *Ancient Pueblo Peoples.* Montreal and Washington D.C.: St. Remy Press and Smithsonian Institution.

Cox, Beverly, and Martin Jacobs. 1991. *Spirit of the Harvest: North American Indian Cooking.* New York: Stewart, Tabori & Chang.

Curtin, L.S.M. 1947. *Healing Herbs of the Upper Rio Grande; Traditional Medicine of the Southwest.* Santa Fe, New Mexico: Western Edge Press.

Cushing, Frank Hamilton. 1920. *Zuni Breadstuff.* Indian Notes and Monographs 8, Museum of the American Indian. New York: Heye Foundation.

Deloria, Vine Jr. 1991. *Sacred Lands and Religious Freedom.* New York: Association on American Indian Affairs.

Epple, Anne Orth. 1995. *Plants of Arizona.* Helena, Mont.: Falcon Publishing.

Eshbaugh, W.H., S.I. Guttman, and M.J. McLeod. "The Origin and Evolution of Domesticated Capsicum Species." *Journal of Ethnobiology* 3 (I): 49–54.

Ford, Richard I. 1985b. *Prehistoric Food Production in North America,* ed. Richard I. Ford. Anthropology Papers 75, Museum of Anthropology. Ann Arbor: University of Michigan.

_____. 1994. "Corn Is Our Mother", in *Corn & Culture; In The Prehistoric New World.* Boulder, Colorado: Westview Press.

Foster, Nelson & Linda S. Cordell, eds. 1992. *Chilies to Chocolate; Food the Americas Gave the World.* Tucson: University of Arizona Press.

Galinat, Walton C. 1985. "Domestication and Diffusion of Maize." In *Prehistoric Food Production in North America,* ed. Richard I. Ford, pp. 245–78. Anthropological Papers 75, Museum of Anthropology. Ann Arbor: University of Michigan.

Harrington, H.D. 1967. *Edible Native Plants of the Rocky Mountains.* Albuquerque: University of New Mexico Press.

Irwin-Williams, Cynthia. 1979. "Post-Pleistocene Archeology, 7000–2000 B.C." In *Handbook of North American Indians, Southwest,* vol. 9, ed. Alfonso Ortiz. Washington: Smithsonian Institution.

Johnson, Sylvia A. 1997. *Tomatoes, Potatoes, Corn, and Beans. How The Foods of The Americas Changed Eating Around The World.* New York: Atheneum Books.

Kaplan, Lawrence, and Lucille N. Kaplan. 1992. "Beans of the Americas." In *Chilies to Chocolate: Food the Americas Gave the World,* ed. Nelson Foster and Linda S. Cordell. Tucson: University of Arizona Press.

Mangelsdorf, Paul C. 1922. *Corn: Its Origin, Evolution and Improvement.* Cambridge, Mass.: Harvard University Press.

Mangelsdorf, Paul C., R.S. MacNeish, and W.C. Galinat. 1956. "Archaeological Evidence on the Diffusion and Evolution of Maize in Northeastern Mexico." *Botanical Museum Leaflets,* vol. 17, no. 5. Cambridge, Mass.: Harvard University.

_____. 1971. "Domestication of Corn." In *Prehistoric Agriculture,* ed. Stuart Struever. Garden City, N.Y.: Natural History Press.

Miller, Mark. 1991. *The Great Chile Book.* Berkeley, California: Ten Speed Press.

Moerman, Daniel E. 1998. *Native American Ethnobotany.* Portland, Oregon: Timber Press.

Moore, Michael. 1979. *Medicinal Plants of the Mountain West.* Santa Fe, New Mexico: Museum of New Mexico Press.

Nabhan, Gary Paul. 1972 "Chiltepines!" In *El Palacio,* Museum of New Mexico 84 (2): 30–34.

_____. 1989. *Enduring Seeds; Native American Agriculture and Wild Plant Conservation.* New York: North Point Press.

Pickersgill, Barbara. 1966. "Migrations of Chili Peppers, *Capsicum* Species, in the Americas." In *Pre-Columbian Plant Migration,* ed. Doris Stone, Cambridge, Mass.: Harvard University Press.

Robbins, Wilfred W., John Peabody Harrington, and Barbara Freire-Marreco. 1916. *Ethnobotany of the Tewa Indians.* Smithsonian Institution Bureau of American Ethnology Bulletin 55, Washington, D.C.

Ross, Winifred. 1941. *The Present Day Dietary Habits of the Papago Indians.* Unpublished master's thesis for the University of Arizona.

Tilford, Gregory L. 1997. *Edible and Medicinal Plants of the West.* Missoula, Montana: Mountain Press Publishing Company.

Weathermax, Paul. 1923. *The Story of the Maize Plant.* Chicago: University of Chicago Press.

ENDNOTES

INTRODUCTION

i. Feld, Steven, and Keith Basso, eds., 1996, *Senses of Place.* Santa Fe, N.M.: School of American Research Press.

ii. Deloria, Vine Jr., 1994, *God is Red; A Native View of Religion.* Golden Colorado: Fulcrum Publishing.

iii. Ortiz, Alfonso, ed., 1979, *Southwest. Handbook of North American Indians.* (Volume 9) General Editor, William C. Sturtevant. Washington D.C.: Smithsonian Institution.

iv. Cordell, Linda S., 1984, *Prehistory of the Southwest.* Orlando, Fla.: Academic Press Inc., and Gunnerson, James H., 1979, "Southern Athapaskan Archeology." In *Handbook of North American Indians, Southwest,* vol. 9, ed. Alfonso Ortiz. Washington D.C.: Smithsonian Institution.

v. Ortiz, Alfonso, ed., 1979, *Southwest. Handbook of North American Indians.* (Volume 9) General Editor, William C. Sturtevant. Washington D.C.: Smithsonian Institution.

vi. Cordell, Linda S., 1984, *Prehistory of the Southwest.* Orlando, Fla.: Academic Press Inc.

vii. Ortiz, Alfonso, ed., 1979, *Southwest. Handbook of North American Indians.* (Volume 9) General Editor, William C. Sturtevant. Washington D.C.: Smithsonian Institution.

viii. Perry, Edgar, 1994, "Beautiful History." In *All Roads Are Good: Native Voices on Life and Culture.* Washington D.C.: Smithsonian Institution Press.

ix. Cooper, Ann, and Lisa M. Holmes, 2000, *Bitter Harvest: A Chef's Perspective on the Hidden Dangers in the Foods We Eat and What You Can Do About It.* New York: Routledge.

x. Ibid.

xi. Walter Whitewater, 2001, personal interview.

CORN: THE ESSENCE OF LIFE

i. Mangelsdorf, Paul C., R.S. MacNeish, and W.C. Galinat, 1964, "Domestication of Corn." *Science,* vol. 143, pp. 538–45.

ii. Coe, Sophie D., 1994, *America's First Cuisines.* Austin: University of Texas Press.

iii. Carter, George F., 1945, "Plant Geography and Culture History in the American Southwest." *Viking Fund Publications in Anthropology* 5:1–140.
Ford, Richard I., 1985a, "Pattern of Prehistoric Food Production in North America." In *Prehistoric Food Production in North America,* ed. Richard I. Ford, pp. 341–64. Anthropological Papers 75, Museum of Anthropology. Ann Arbor: University of Michigan.
Galinat, Walton C., 1985, "Domestication and Diffusion of Maize." In *Prehistoric Food Production in North America,* ed. Richard I. Ford, pp. 245–78. Anthropological Papers 75, Museum of Anthropology. Ann Arbor: University of Michigan.
González, José Jesús Sánchez, 1994, "Modern Variability and Patterns of Maize Movement in Mesoamerica." In *Corn & Culture in the Prehistoric New World,* pp. 135–56. Boulder, Colorado: Westview Press Inc.

iv. Bohrer, Vorsila L., 1995, "The Where, When and Why of the Corn Guardians." In *Soil, Water, Biology and Belief in Prehistoric and Traditional Southwestern Agriculture.* New Mexico Archaeological Council. Special Publication 2, pp. 361–68.
Mangelsdorf, Paul C., and Robert Gatlin Reeves, 1939, *The Origins of Indian Corn and its Relatives.* College Station: Texas Agricultural Experiment Station.

v. Talaswaima, Terrance, 1978, "Hopi Creation Story as Told by Terrance Talaswaima, Hopi Artist from Second Mesa." In *Mother Corn.* Video recording, KBYU-TV Provo, Utah: Native American Public Broadcasting Consortium.
Coughlin, Donald, 1982, *Corn is Life.* Video recording, Tellens, Inc.
Courlander, Harold, 1970, *People of the Short Blue Corn: Tales and Legends of the Hopi Indians.* New York: Harcourt Brace Jovanovich.

vi. Coe, Sophie D., 1994, *America's First Cuisines.* Austin: University of Texas Press.

vii. Hawke, Sharryl Davis, and James E. Davis, 1992, *Seeds of Change: The Story of Cultural Exchange after 1492.* Menlo Park, California: Addison-Wesley Publishing Co.
Galinat, Walton C., 1994, "Maize: Gift from America's First Peoples." In *Chilies to Chocolate: Food the Americas Gave the World.* Tucson: University of Arizona Press.
Barreiro, José, ed., 1989, *Indian Corn of the Americas, Gift to the World.* Volume VI, Nos. 1 & 2, Spring/Summer. Cornell University, Northeast Indian Quarterly.

viii. Ortiz, Alfonso, 1994, "Some Cultural Meanings of Corn in Aboriginal North American", in *Corn & Culture; In The Prehistoric New World,* pp. 527–44.

ix. Buskirk, Winfred, 1949, *Western Apache Subsistence Economy.* Unpublished Ph.D. dissertation for the University of New Mexico.

Castetter, Edward, and Ruth Underhill, 1935, "Ethnobiological Studies in the American Southwest II: Ethnobiology of the Papago Indians." *Bulletin: University of New Mexico,* vol. 4, no. 3.

Ortiz, Alfonso, 1994, "Some Cultural Meanings of Corn in Aboriginal North American", in *Corn & Culture; In The Prehistoric New World,* pp. 527–44.

Spier, Leslie, 1933, *Yuman Tribes of the Gila River,* Chicago: University of Chicago Press.

x. Ortiz, Alfonso, 1994, "Some Cultural Meanings of Corn in Aboriginal North American", in *Corn & Culture; In The Prehistoric New World,* pp. 527–44.

Underhill, Ruth, 1938, *Singing for Power.* Berkeley: University of California Press.

xi. Kavena, Juanita Tiger, 1980, *Hopi Cookery.* Tucson: University of Arizona Press.

xii. Ibid.

CHILES: THE SPICE OF LIFE

i. Coe, Sophie D., 1994, *America's First Cuisines.* Austin: University of Texas Press.

ii. Coe, Sophie D., 1994, *America's First Cuisines.* Austin: University of Texas Press.

iii. Andrews, Jean, 1992, "The Peripatetic Chili Pepper: Diffusion of the Domesticated Capsicums Since Columbus." In *Chilies to Chocolate: Food the Americas Gave the World,* eds. Nelson Foster and Linda S. Cordell. Tucson: University of Arizona Press.

iv. Cordell, Linda S., 1984, *Prehistory of the Southwest.* Orlando, Fla.: Academic Press Inc.

v. Andrews, Jean, 1992, "The Peripatetic Chili Pepper: Diffusion of the Domesticated Capsicums Since Columbus." In *Chilies to Chocolate: Food the Americas Gave the World,* eds. Nelson Foster and Linda S. Cordell. Tucson: University of Arizona Press.

GROWN FROM THE VINE: TOMATOES, SQUASH, PUMPKINS, AND MELONS

i. Cordell, Linda S., 1984, *Prehistory of the Southwest.* Orlando, Fla.: Academic Press Inc.

ii. MacNeish, Richard S., 1958, "Preliminary Archaeological Investigations in the Sierra de Tamaulipos, Mexico." *Transactions of the American Philosophical Society,* vol. 48, pt. 6. Philadelphia.

_____, 1967, "A Summary of the Subsistence." In *Environment and Subsistence: The Prehistory of the Tehuacan Valley* (Vol. 1), ed. Douglas S. Byers, pp. 290-309. Austin: University of Texas Press.

iii. MacNeish, Richard S., 1967, "A Summary of the Subsistence." In *Environment and Subsistence: The Prehistory of the Tehuacan Valley* (Vol. 1), ed. Douglas S. Byers, pp. 290–309. Austin: University of Texas Press

iv. Ford, Richard I., 1981, "Gardening and Farming before A.D. 1000: Patterns of Prehistoric Cultivation North of Mexico." *Journal of Ethnobiology* 1 (1): 6–27

v. Coe, Sophie D., 1994, *America's First Cuisines.* Austin: University of Texas Press.

vi. Ibid.

vii. Kavena, Juanita Tiger, 1980, *Hopi Cookery.* Tucson: University of Arizona Press.

viii. Coe, Sophie D., 1994, *America's First Cuisines.* Austin: University of Texas Press.

ix. Whiting, Alfred, 1966, *Ethnobotany of the Hopi.* Flagstaff, Ariz.: Northland Press.

NATIVE HARVEST: WILD GREENS, CACTI, FRUITS, AND HERBS

i. Neithammer, Carolyn, 1999, *American Indian Cooking: Recipes from the Southwest.* Lincoln: Bison Books, University of Nebraska Press.

ii. Nabhan, Gary Paul, 1985, *Gathering the Desert.* Tucson: University of Arizona Press.

iii. Martin, Paul Schultz, 1963, *The Last 10,000 Years: A Fossil Pollen Record of the American Southwest.* Tucson: University of Arizona Press.

iv. Cordell, Linda S., 1984, *Prehistory of the Southwest.* Orlando, Fla.: Academic Press Inc.

v. Dunmire, William W., and Gail D. Tierney, 1995, *Wild Plants of the Pueblo Province: Exploring Ancient and Enduring Uses.* Santa Fe: Museum of New Mexico Press.

vi. Bell, Willis H., and Edward F. Castetter, 1941, "Ethnobiological Studies in the American Southwest VII: The Utilization of Yucca, Sotol and Beargrass by the Aborigines in the American Southwest." *University of New Mexico Bulletin,* vol. 5, no. 5, Biological Series.

vii. Dunmire, William W., and Gail D. Tierney, 1995, *Wild Plants of the Pueblo Province: Exploring Ancient and Enduring Uses.* Santa Fe: Museum of New Mexico Press.

SUSTENANCE IN A POD: BEANS, NUTS, AND SEEDS

i. MacNeish, Richard S., 1958, "Preliminary Archaeological Investigations in the Sierra de Tamaulipos, Mexico." *Transactions of the American Philosophical Society,* vol. 48, pt. 6. Philadelphia.

ii. Cordell, Linda S., 1984, *Prehistory of the Southwest.* Orlando, Fla.: Academic Press Inc.

iii. Ford, Richard I., 1981, "Gardening and Farming before A.D. 1000: Patterns of Prehistoric Cultivation North of Mexico." *Journal of Ethnobiology* 1 (1): 6–27

iv. Castetter, Edward, and Willis H. Bell, 1942, *Pima and Papago Indian Agriculture.* Albuquerque: University of New Mexico Press.

v. Cordell, Linda S., 1984, *Prehistory of the Southwest.* Orlando, Fla.: Academic Press Inc.

vi. Kaplan, Lawrence, and Lucille N. Kaplan, 1992, "Beans of the Americas." In *Chilies to Chocolate: Food the Americas Gave the World,* eds. Nelson Foster and Linda S. Cordell. Tucson: University of Arizona Press.

vii. Dunmire, William W., and Gail D. Tierney, 1995, *Wild Plants of the Pueblo Province: Exploring Ancient and Enduring Uses.* Santa Fe: Museum of New Mexico Press.

viii. Ibid.

THE LAND'S CREATURES: GAME BIRDS, MEATS, AND FISH

i. Cordell, Linda S., 1984, *Prehistory of the Southwest.* Orlando, Fla.: Academic Press Inc.

ii. Basso, Keith, 1970, The Cibecue Apache. New York: Holt, Rinehart, and Winston.

INDEX

INDEX

INDEX

INDEX

INDEX